P9-DWK-659

To Jackie !
Congratulations on becoming the
7th minister of UU of Laramie.
Enjoy this as you can - and share
it as you wish. See card for
my other books - all published
this year. Maybe, it's about time,
Loh!

Exploring
The Soul -
And
Brother Jesus

Greatly,
Will
Bessler
742-6868

Francis William Bessler

(Compiled in 2015)

Copyright © 2015 Francis William Bessler
All rights reserved.

ISBN: 1514243040
ISBN 13: 9781514243046
Library of Congress Control Number: 2015909214
CreateSpace Independent Publishing Platform
North Charleston, South Carolina

A Composite of
Past Philosophical Writings
featuring
Essays & Songs
including
a work on the soul called
UNMASKING THE SOUL (1988)
&
a *CHILD OF HUMANITY*
Essay Series (2005)

Dedicated to
ALL OF US
because
ALL OF US
are the same.
It is only
thinking we are different
that causes
most of our ills.

Copyrighted by
Francis William Bessler
Laramie, Wyoming, U.S.A.
June, 2015

Preface

Note:
Following this Preface, I will offer an additional summary of this work as prepared for a book review that I wrote for the publishers of this work - Create Space.

We all have our own ideas about the soul - even if we don't believe in a soul. I guess if we do not believe in a soul, our idea about the soul is that it is an illusion. Still, others of us have an idea that somehow the soul really exists as an independent entity - that is, independent of the body. Those of us who believe such, however, disagree as to how the soul must originate - and what the destiny of the soul is - perhaps regardless of how it originates.

I must admit that when I was younger, I believed that God creates each individual soul; but looking out and about at Creation and Humanity within Creation, in time, I came to suspect that idea. It became clear to me that bodies are not created by God because they have a "natural" explanation. Related to God, it became clear to me that God is not my body's personal creator. In general, I guess you could say that Nature is my body's Creator.

But what about my soul? **Could it be that God is a Personal Creator of my soul - or can there be another explanation?** In 1979 and 1980, in my late '30s, I became somewhat obsessed with the soul. I read quite a few books on the subject, but none satisfied me - including the idea of my youth that God creates the soul. Nothing I read or reviewed convinced me that anyone really knew (or knows) the truth. I was left in a quandary.

As it happened, in the Fall of 1980, I was walking in a City Park in Denver, Colorado, thinking about the soul and still wondering about it. Then I chanced upon a mother duck with several little ducklings following after her - and it hit me that if I have a soul, it probably has to follow that pattern of a parent-child relationship. What did a mama duck and her kids tell me? They told me that if I have a soul, it has to come from another soul. Voila! There was the answer for which I had been searching for several years. Given the pattern of natural beginnings, if souls exist at all, originally, they have to come from other souls - not from a Personal Creator God. Like those little ducklings came from their Mama Duck, and like all babies come from their mothers, so, too, it must be with souls - if they exist at all. Well, it was a start anyway. At least, it made a lot more sense than any of the other ideas I had reviewed.

That idea of a *"natural soul"* came to me in my late '30s; but in my late '40s, in late 1988, I decided I needed to write a book about the soul and investigate the various theories about it - as well as propose my own idea of a *natural soul*. The result was a book I called *SOULS -*

ILLUSIONS OR REALITIES? After I finished with it, I tried to find a book publisher, but I found only one who expressed any interest - Winston-Derek located in Nashville, Tennessee. In 1989 or 1990, I visited with one Robert Earl, who was the chief editor of Winston-Derek productions - and he and I agreed to collaborate. Winston-Derek would pay for printing 1,000 copies of my book - and I would pay for printing another 1,000. Then Winston-Derek would feature my work in book stores they had around the country.

I must say I was excited. Robert Earl told me that he thought my book would become the "corner stone" of future Winston-Derek publications. We signed a contract according to the terms Robert and I arranged - and then, Robert Earl suddenly died. I never found out the reason for his death, but the subsequent chief editor was appalled at my book because he thought it challenged the thoughts of all the other Winston-Derek writers - who were all traditionally Christian based. So, just like that, the new chief editor decided that Winston-Derek would agree to print my 1,000 copies since I had already paid them to do it, but they would not collaborate with me to print 1,000 books on their own at their expense - and they would not feature my book in their book stores.

After that, since the early '90s, I have kept my book to myself; but in 2003, I decided to rewrite it a bit and change the name from *SOULS - ILLUSIONS OR REALITIES?* to *UNMASKING THE SOUL*; and now, I am including it in this work - along with an essay series I wrote in 2005 called a *CHILD OF HUMANITY SERIES.*

I will let that series speak for itself; but it is really about listening to the *Jesus of THE GOSPEL OF MARY MAGDALENE* and finding meaning in life by pursuing the *"child of humanity"* within us. That series featured a few songs that I wrote to help punctuate the essays - and they will be included as well.

To complete this work, I am featuring a poetic commentary with refrain that I called **SONG OF MY DIVINE NATURISM** that I wrote in 2004. I consider myself a *"Divine Naturist"* - my own term - for believing that **All Nature is Divine** - including all of us within Nature. I do believe there are many *"Divine Naturists"* in this world, even though, since I coined the term, not many would call themselves by such a title. Perhaps, in time, a lot of "hidden" *Divine Naturists* will come forward and claim the title for themselves - if they believe that the commentary within my song suits them; but regardless of title, I do believe there are many in this world who are really *Divine Naturists* - maybe yourself included.

Also, I am including a recent essay and song I have just written about each of us being of solitary worth. At the front end of this work, see a recent essay called *AN ISLAND MENTALITY* and a recent poem/song called *An Island Unto Myself.*

If you like what you read here, you may enjoy other of my writings as well. In late 2012, I started my own website that includes all of my past writings as well as ongoing blogs of current thought. In August of 2014, I printed a number of recent essays written previously as blogs - along with a few songs. That work is called **WILD FLOWERS** - and it is available - as this one is - on Amazon.com.

Down through the years, I have also written a few philosophical type stories - and just recently, I decided to combine five of those in a work called **FIVE HEAVEN ON EARTH STORIES**. That work, too, is available on Amazon.com. In time, I will publish all of my songs (about 200) in a single work - and it, too, will be available on Amazon.com - probably by the end of this year - 2015 - if not sooner. After that, I intend to publish a **WILD FLOWERS # 2** - probably as soon as I finish with my book of my songs and poems - perhaps by the Fall of 2015. After that, who knows?

For any of my works, check out works and links at my website - www.una-bella-vita.com.

Briefly about myself, I was born on a small farm outside of Powell, Wyoming on December 3rd, 1941 - the seventh of eight children of Leo and Clara Bessler. I was raised Christian Catholic and even spent 6 years after high school graduation in 1960 from Powell High studying for the Catholic ministry - starting in the Fall of 1960 at St. Lawrence Seminary in Mount Calvary, Wisconsin, to learn Latin - as a requirement to continue studies at St. Thomas Seminary in Denver, Colorado. In the Fall of 1961, with a Latin education behind me, I entered St. Thomas Seminary.

I loved all of my seminary years, but in the Spring of 1966, I was "discontinued" from further studies at St. Thomas because "your thinking is not that of a Catholic priest." At least, that is what I was told by the Rector of St. Thomas - one, Father Danagher - when I was told I was being terminated from further study. My main offense was that I argued that *Faith must be subject to Understanding* - or else we could never be certain of any dogma upheld as truth. My Church disagreed with that and my Dogma professor even labeled me as a "heretic" for making Faith subject to Understanding; but I still believe it today.

Subsequent to my seminary training, I have led quite a life - bearing out what Father Danagher told me long ago - that "my thinking is not that of a Catholic priest." As my writings below will attest, Father Danagher was right. If you wish to know more about me, I will refer you to my website (see above and below) - which will bear more of my biography.

With that, let me leave you to my ideas about the soul in this work - and other ideas about the ideal of finding the "*child of humanity*" within us. Life is not near as complicated as we might think it is. I do believe that **BROTHER JESUS** - not **Lord Jesus** - tried to convey that message 2,000 years ago; but we failed to hear it - probably because we were not open to hear such a message. We were not looking for a *"Brother Jesus."* We were looking for a **"Messiah Jesus."** Are we open to approaching Jesus as a brother today? That remains to be seen; but let's hope so.

Thanks to Everyone who have been with me along the way; and Thanks to All who choose to read this effort.

For sure, we are all in this wonderful thing called Life together. *Brothers and Sisters are we all! Don't you agree?*

A special thanks is in order, though, to my current companion, Nancy Shaw. Nancy is 82 as I write this; and I am 73. In early 2012, Nancy's husband of over 30 years, Joce, passed at the age of 88 due to Parkinson's Disease. Joce and I were good friends and were "walking buddies" for awhile before Joce passed. I do believe Joce would have enjoyed this work because he and I were of the same mind about spiritually related issues, generally speaking. Since Joce's passing, Nancy, his wife, and I have bonded. Nancy is only one day older than my oldest living sister, Rita. Nancy was born on Nov. 22nd, 1932; and Rita was born on Nov. 23rd of that same year. So, let me dedicate this work - not only to Nancy - but to her good friend and mine, her late husband, Joce.

Thanks!

Francis William Bessler
Laramie, Wyoming
www.una-bella-vita.com
May 23rd, 2015

Another Summary

This work is mostly ideas about the soul and ideas about Jesus - with a special emphasis on original ideas about the soul and about Jesus as consistent with those original ideas about the soul. Almost all of this book is comprised of works written in the past, but only compiled together in this one book. My ideas on the soul were originally written in 1988 and my ideas about Jesus were written in 2005, but both works are included in this one compilation.

I have long believed that understanding the soul is critical to understanding anything of importance - including anything about luminaries of history - like Jesus. I do believe that so many truth seekers have simply assumed that what others have believed about the soul is the truth and then have patterned their lives based on those assumptions.

I have tried to not assume that others have been right about their ideas about the soul and have insisted that I find my own answers about the soul. Accordingly, my perception of life has been considerably different than that of most ancients because my ideas about the soul have turned out different.

In my book, I examine various traditional ideas about the **"assumed origin"** of the soul and analyze what the ramifications of those ideas might be. Then I offer an *original idea* that deals with the **"probable"** origin of the soul and perhaps, destiny of the soul. In not basing my ideas about the origin and destiny of a soul according to various traditional theories of the soul, I think I have something unique to offer the world - though I did not pursue a different explanation of the soul for the sake of the world, but for me alone. Indeed, my answers are my own, but I do not mind sharing them with others; and that is what my book tries to do.

In a second part of my book, I try to offer a different explanation for Jesus other than being a **"Jewish Messiah"** simply because the idea of messiah in the first place is based on an explanation of the soul that is contrary to my own conclusions.

My idea of the soul is that each soul occupies a body by virtue of *personal selection,* not **imposed infusion,** so to speak. Most traditionalists act like the soul is somehow "infused" into a body by virtue of **"Divine Mandate** or **Divine Selection** or **Divine Process"** and therefore each soul is subject to **"Divine Judgment."**

Jesus has been offered as a **"Divine Judge"** by those who believe in such an explanation of the soul; but my ideas about the soul do not require either Divine Selection or Divine Judgment of the soul. Therefore, I have had to offer a different interpretation of Jesus - if I want to treasure a story of Jesus at all. In not needing any "Divine Judge" at all, Jesus can only be understood as a fellow human - or *brother.* If a **Divine Judge** is not needed because souls are not created by a **Divine God,** then *Jesus* can only be understood as a *"brother"* and not a **"Lord."**

In the banned gospels of **Thomas and Mary Magdalene,** banned since the 4th Century by a Church that offers Divine Selection and Divine Judgment, I have found an explanation of Jesus other than that of Jewish Messiah or Divine Judge. In the second part of this book, I speculate a bit about my alternate different view of Jesus - using various verses of *The Gospels of Thomas and Mary* to do that.

In addition, a few songs that I have written about the soul and life in general are also included - especially a final song and commentary called ***SONG OF MY DIVINE NATURISM***. I consider myself to be a *"Divine Naturist"* in that ***I Believe that an Infinite God must be IN all*** - thus making all Divine by virtue of that Presence.

In general, though, perhaps some will find my "different speculations" about the soul and Jesus useful; and that is why I have taken the effort to share them in this one rather small book. Enjoy them as you will.

Thanks!

Francis William Bessler
June 5th, 2015

Contents

An Island Mentality

By
Francis William Bessler
Laramie, Wyoming
4/12/2015

I like to think of birth and death as one movement, as one overall process, as it were. It becomes so clear to me when I do that. If I imagine Mom & Dad on some island before I was born, it becomes even clearer. I like to think of such pondering as being somewhat of *An Island Mentality,* so to speak. There Mom is about to give me birth - and no one else is around, but Dad. Out I come from Mom's womb - and there I am as a new baby of the world.

Now - given that Dad & Mom & me are on some island and have been so since time began, so to speak - we would not have been exposed to any other traditions or rituals of the human race. I guess you could say we would have been free to decide for ourselves about life; and why not? Just imagine! No tradition to scope us or scold us. There we are - free to figure it out all by ourselves.

But let me go back to another moment - a time of my conception in the womb of my mother. Mom & Dad have just linked and out of that linkage, I began. My soul came into the picture, though, separate from this happening on our little island. From some Paranormal Location, my soul entered into this little embryo, just "created" by Mom & Dad.

Realistically, now, would it have been likely that my body would have been conceived in some degree of sin - or separation from God? That is what sin is - according to all those many traditions and religions out there in the rest of the world - but not on our island. Somehow, little Sonny - or Sonny's body - is supposed to have been conceived and born in sin - according to main land traditions and religions; but how could that be? How could Mom & Dad being together be a matter of sin? Where is the proof of such a silly notion?

And so little Sonny grows in Mom's womb and there comes a time when he is born. Out he comes! Is it a Miracle or a Sin? Now, given that Mom & Dad have not been exposed to all sort of tradition and religion on main lands, it is inconceivable to me that Dad or Mom would consider that their giving birth to me is a matter of impropriety or sin.

Alright, that is my beginning - on my imagined island of purity. Unaware of anything else happening in the world, I grow. In time, I become an adult myself - just like Mom & Dad. Then Mom dies - and Dad and me grieve, but we don't wonder that Mom's soul has gone on to some land of punishment for just being herself. Wherever it is that Mom has gone - or Mom's soul has gone - hey, it must be as good as the island where we all lived. Why not?

Then Dad dies - and I am left all alone. It would have been nice if some lovely lady had come along and I could have mated, but in this little imagining, we - Mom, Dad, and me - have been alone. They have gone on now to whatever comes after death, but there is no reason for me to believe that their destinies could be anything other than splendid. Remember now - in this little imagining, neither Dad, nor Mom, nor me have had any exposure to main land thinking. We have been left to ourselves - and we have pondered alone - with our *"Island Mentality."*

Eventually, I become old myself and pass away. No one would be around to mourn me or celebrate me. No grave, nothing left behind but whatever plant, fish, bird, and animal habitation that had been our blessing while we lived on our island.

When Mom died, Dad and I took her body and propped it up against a tree - just so we could remember her. When Dad died, I propped his bones up against a tree near where Mom was propped; but when I died, no one was around to prop me up. Knowing that no one would be around to prop me up, I might have decided to die propped up, right next to Mom & Dad.

Now imagine that sometime after I might have died, a little ship docks at our little island. There we are seen - Mom & Dad & me - propped up against three trees;

that is, our skeletons are so propped; and those visitors who come ashore might wonder who we had been.

But would it have mattered who we might have been? We lived on an Island in Paradise. We knew nothing of sin or having inherited some terrible disgrace. We lived in innocence. We prospered in innocence; and we died in innocence. No one was around to make us do otherwise.

Now, take Dad & Mom & me onto some main land and into some main land tradition. Why should we have acted any different than we did on our little island - surrounded with wonderful mystery amidst a Fantastic Creation? Personally, I don't think we should have acted any different on a main land than we did on our little island; and I do believe that is the key to knowing the truth.

Think for yourself; and do not let anyone tell you what you have no need or desire to know. That is what I call living according to an *"Island Mentality."* I think I have been doing it for most of my life; and for what it's worth, I highly recommend it.

An Island Unto Myself

By
Francis William Bessler
Laramie, Wyoming
5/8/2015

I am an island unto myself;
and, so, my friend, are you.
That is only to say that within myself,
I can find the truth.
That is so because
Everything is Divine;
and to look at anyone or thing
is for All Life to find.

I am an island unto myself;
all I need is to look at me.
There are, of course, other islands,
but all are the same as me.
We differ in our detail,
but in worth we are the same;
and so for me to look at me
is to find everyone in that place.

I'm an island unto myself.
No one else is needed to confirm.
All I see are other selves
from a bird to a worm.
We are all in this thing of Life;
and together we should act.
But you be you and I'll be me;
and equality will be our pact.

I'm an island unto myself
because I'm as sacred as anyone.
An Infinite God must be in me;
and that's why my life should be fun.
It should not matter where I am
because All is Divine.
To see otherwise, my friend,
is to go through life as blind.

I'm an island unto myself.
So, let me enjoy my diversity.
And let me look at you
and let me know integrity.
Integrity is only looking at the whole
and knowing each member is of God.
To be at peace is to treat all as one
and to know that all deserve applause.

I'm an island unto myself.
I'm like a tiny seed
that can grow into a wondrous flower
or into a gigantic tree.
To plant a seed and watch it grow
is to become aware
that no matter what we are,
Divinity must be there.

So, come with me
to my island unto myself
and find that no one is an island
if compassion is what is felt.
Love truly abides on any island
if we *Live Our Values Everyday;*
and every mainland is like an island
if we but treat it that away.

UNMASKING THE SOUL!

By
Francis William Bessler

**Originally Written in
December of 1988.**

Revised in 2003 & 2005.

A similar version was previously
Copyrighted by the same author
in Atlanta, Ga. U.S.A. in 1990
Under the title of
SOULS – ILLUSIONS OR REALITIES

**Dedicated to My Parent Soul or Souls
and to any Child Souls I may have in the future
and to all who have encouraged me
in my search for the Truth of the Soul.**

Contents

Introduction

Ladies and Gentlemen and little adults, let me tell you about this work. It is an investigation of the soul – that is, an investigation of the various major theories of the soul. There are several pet theories or beliefs of the soul that will be investigated. Perhaps, and quite likely, your own belief will be among them. An original concept or theory called *"The Natural Soul Theory"* will also be discussed. I hope you enjoy the discussion and find it worthwhile.

What are my credentials for writing on the soul? It's hard to say. I have no degrees. My only claim to authenticity is a lifelong dedication to find the truth about the soul. Perhaps there is a good deal of insight behind my thoughts – or maybe just luck.

For what it's worth, I studied for the Catholic ministry for six years in Wisconsin and Colorado after graduating from high school in Powell, Wyoming in 1960. I conjectured about the soul a lot during those years. Disliking a lot of the doctrines of the Church, however, I discontinued my studies for the ministry in 1966 and left the Church completely in 1973.

Much of the cause of my disenchantment with the Church was its perception of the soul. That discord led me to search for something more agreeable; however, it would not be until 1980 that I would finish my own personal search; for in that year, I found, or discovered, the truth for which I sought for so long. It is that truth, or perception of the truth, that is the kernel of this work on the soul. Perhaps it's only one man's journey and cannot apply to anyone else, but I do not believe that. I think my own journey can be shared; and that's what I am trying to do with this work.

With that in mind, let us begin.

Francis William Bessler
Laramie, Wyoming, U.S.A.
September 22nd, 2005

1

The Soul as Illusion

Soul, of course, can mean different things to different people. It means only "representative being" for some. My soul is my inner being. Poetically, it's the heart of me. For sure, it is that for me too, but it is also much more.

For some, it lives only as long as the body lives. It is, then, part and partial of the body. Its life originates from the body and has no sustenance outside of it. For those who believe this way, the soul is truly an illusion, not a reality unto itself. Soul becomes equated with attitude and philosophy and approach to life. It is not an entity unto itself.

One of my best friends believed in this definition of the soul. I say, believed, because he is past tense now. He has passed on to what he believed is oblivion. My friend, Emmett Needham, was a kind man; and I think I have never had a better friend. I know I have never had a better friend.

I have often wondered how he could be so kind and gentle by believing as he did in mortality of the soul. Why didn't he just go out and be the meanest person he could be and take what he could while he lived? If he had no fear of a judgment after life, what difference did it make?

Many would have done just that – plundered, murdered, raped, anything at all to get what they wanted because there is so little time to live it up, but not my friend, Emmett. Though life was mortal in his eyes, he wasn't about to squander it on meanness. He saw meanness as squandering life by being insensitive to its wonders.

Emmett stood in awe of Nature and embraced everything about it and everyone in it. Within his circle of friends, and I have never known anyone who had more, Emmett was a kind of saint and would have been preferred 10 to 0 over a traditional hard nosed saint like, for instance, Paul of Tarsus. Saint Emmett saw simplicity through kindness as the answer to the good life. Saint Paul saw complexity through judgment as the answer to the good life – and punishment for those who don't measure up to some strict standard.

Beside Emmett, I have known others, too, who had no belief in an after life of the soul. Quite frankly, I love the people I have known who believe this way. At least in my friend, Emmett, fear of life and even fear of rejection and dying were absent because he saw his life and his living as being in the long stretch of things, rather insignificant. Most people I have known cannot survive happily unless they view themselves as significant. Most never do. So they live unhappy lives.

Emmett lived a fairly happy life, bless his soul, because he did not depend upon significance for virtue. Those of us souls who do depend upon significance or being recognized often pay a mighty price of being ignored for that dependency; and in the long run, we should ask, is it worth it? Who am I anyway that I should deserve admiration? Is not the nature of my being the real father of my attraction and my blessings?

Can consciousness itself be explained as only physical and chemical processes and reactions? Those who believe that the soul exists only as an illusion must also believe this. Intelligence and emotion must also be explained within these boundaries. Is my intelligence the expression of the brain of my body? Are my emotions solely the expression of touching and being touched – like electrical impulses that come and go, dependent upon the position of a switch? Is the soul confined to expression within the limits of a yes or no reality? Yes, I'm being touched and it feels good. Yes, I'm being touched, but it does not feel good. I'm not being touched and I do not like the inattention; or I am not being touched and I don't want to be.

Is touching and being touched, then, the major graciousness of life, its basic reward? Are wars between good and evil total nonsense? In the view of this concept that the soul is solely an illusion, evil and the struggle between it and good are voids. Neither the evil nor the struggle actually exists. When the body dies, there is no judgment; so when the body lives, there can be no evil; for in the final analysis, evil can only exist as the judgment of life. Where there is no life hereafter, neither can there be judgment.

At an earlier point in my life, I would have been repulsed by the very thought that I am only mortal, that my soul is also my body or a process of it; but since Emmett and a few others I have known like him, I have lost a fear of that possibility. What a wonderful notion it is that judgment need not be feared for lack of a life hereafter to be judged. For those who truly believe this, living cannot be burdened with idiotic fears that have no base in reality because life itself is the only reality of perception. Life is not divided into regions of good and evil. It just is; and what it is is nothing short of mysterious and miraculous.

Is my friend, Emmett, a saint of his belief? I think so; though I also think he survived and survives as an entity itself. Is my friend, Emmett, in the hell of another's opposing belief? Because he did not believe he had to believe in evil and did not embrace a prince of salvation he did not need, is he condemned for eternity? Is believing only in goodness a sin? Is believing in the sanctity of creation itself grounds for condemnation? Perhaps only a fool of the greatest stature believes it is so.

If I should not believe in an afterlife and then die to find one, is it reasonable to suspect that my non-belief would be grounds for punishment by believers? Should a true prince of goodness and kindness find grace in banning me for my non-belief to a pit of unending hurt? Only a fool would believe it.

Belief itself cannot be grounds for salvation anymore than non-belief can be grounds for punishment. Whether I believe or I do not believe in an afterlife, in the final analysis, it's only kindness that matters because only kindness carries with it the security of insignificance and a gratitude for being.

2

The Soul as Real Entity – Introduction

For some, the soul is an illusion. For others, of course, it is not. For some, like me, the soul is a real entity unto itself. It is an entity unto itself that may marry in time with a body in the span of a human life and may separate with the body upon the death of the body. The remainder of this work will concentrate on that definition of the soul; and we will take an analytical look at several theories regarding this perception of it.

Our discussion, however, is not going to be on the substance of the soul, but rather on the origin of it. Personally, I do not think that in a million years of study that we could begin to define the substance of the soul. In a way, that would be like trying to define the substance of God.

I am not saying that the soul is like God as a synonym or comparable entity. I am just saying the soul and God are both greatly indefinable within the limitations of the human mind. Both the soul and God are invisible and immeasurable and are properly assumed to exist because the alternatives of no God and no soul are almost unimaginable, at least for many of us.

My approach, then, in this little work on the soul is that, assuming the soul exists as an independent entity, what must be its origin? My thinking here is that if we can deduce probable origin, we can also predict probable destiny; and that is really the basic interest in the soul anyway. There are indeed subtle indicators that the soul does exist as an independent entity, and we will touch on a few of them in our discussion, but in the main, we will be talking probable origin and destiny.

Our discussion will focus on two traditional explanations of the origin of the soul and on one somewhat original explanation. Our first discussion will focus on the basic religious doctrine that the soul is directly created by God. Our second discussion will focus on a couple of traditional reincarnation theories of the soul. Then we will deal with an original concept I call *"The Natural Soul Theory."* I have also dubbed my theory *"The Parent Soul Theory."*

Granted that this work is mostly about the origin of the soul and not the substance of the soul, I do offer a sort of definition of the soul as I see it in Part 6 where I discuss the issues that I think my own theory or explanation of the soul resolves that other theories do not. But for preferring to concentrate on the origin of the soul rather than the substance or what of the soul, I will leave my own definition of the soul itself until later.

With that in mind, let us continue.

3

The Soul as

Direct Creation of God

When did I begin? That is, when did my soul begin? If we are to believe those who believe that my soul was instantaneously created by God, I suppose that my soul was instantaneously created sometime between the conception of my body and the birth of it. For those who believe in the direct creation by God theory, however, I do not think that timing is much of an issue. God creates the soul and that is all there is to that – regardless of when it happens.

A serious searcher for the truth of the soul, however, must care and must ask questions to satisfy a healthy and rightful curiosity. Does God wake up when human parents unite to conceive new life and then cooperates like a being in bondage to satisfy the creation of a new soul? Or is it possible some bodies are denied souls?

Is it possible that God will challenge a situation and say, sorry, I'm not giving this one a soul? Is that an explanation of evil, a body not blessed with a soul from God? Does God participate in some cases and fail to participate in others? In the one where He does participate, we have good; and in those cases where He doesn't, we have evil? Such is the burden of those born without souls – to wander forever without the blessing of God?

In my frank opinion, the direct creation explanation of the origin of the soul has more snafus than a field of a thousand **mind bombs**. The serious student of the soul must study the implications and probable conclusions of every theory or concept of the soul. Everywhere you go with the theory of direct creation by God, you end in an explosion.

If God creates a soul for each body, does He decide for the parents to get together and consummate? If so, he automatically gives His blessing to every union, be it within marriage or outside of it, within race or outside of it, be it a teen or a senior citizen; and if God should approve of a twelve year old conceiving, who are we to condemn it? Is it our right to sit in judgment of God?

Many will say, No, it's not right to sit in judgment of God, but God has the right to sit in judgment of us and hand out fate at His whim. Thus He has the right to create one soul trapped in bondage and another blessed in freedom. He has the right to create one soul and give it an inheritance of puritanical restriction and the right to create another soul and give it an inheritance of open splendor. God is all wise and He knows what's best for each soul; and it's up to each soul to suffer or enjoy its own personal fate or fortune. How many mind bombs have already exploded? And we have only begun the investigation of the natural conclusions of this explanation of the soul.

And after the soul is directly created, what does it do – live forever? It begins in time, yet it has no end? Any mathematician will tell you that if an event has no end, it also had no beginning; for where there is no end, there can be no beginning. But the soul has a beginning; therefore, it has to have an ending. If that is the case, where does it end and who ends it? I suppose since only God can create a soul, only He can "uncreate" it. Will He end it for some and extend it for others? And how long will He let us live – a year, a life, a thousand lives, a million lives?

How many mind bombs have we exploded? Why quit now? Let's explode a few more. Let's consider punishment for a soul created by God. Those who believe in this concept generally embrace a thousand fold, punishment for the soul, that is, external punishment. Which soul is to be punished and which one isn't? That's easy. The one who does His will should escape punishment and the one who rebels should not. But what is His will? How do I know it?

I'm told the prophets have been born to receive His will and pass it on to the rest of us poor sinners. Who is the right prophet and how will I recognize him or her? The mind bombs continue to explode, one after another. Everywhere you step, you end up without a leg to stand on. The rightful prophet is the one who speaks the truth. Everyone knows that. Alright, how do I know what is spoken is the truth? By accuracy of happening or prediction, I am told.

Is that to say, then, that if I predict twelve things to happen and they do, by design or otherwise, I can assume that a thirteenth one that can't be verified, like eternal happiness, has to be true? Am I to presume that you are a prophet of God because you always tell the truth? Is the truth something that is a sign of God? Or can an enemy agent tell the truth too? Am I to conclude that you are sent from God because you claim the mission? Does claiming it make it so? The mind bombs continue to explode.

OK, say you are a prophet and I rebel. My soul is condemned, but to what? Fire, you say. Is that to say that the soul can suffer physical harm because the body can? No, that's only a graphical illustration of what's in store for a rebel, you say. He or she won't actually burn because an immaterial soul can't burn, but his or her pain will be like an endless fire. Oh, I see, I say.

And where will this soul of mine be burned by something that's like fire but is not fire? In Hell, you say. And where is Hell? Is there a section of God's great universe that He has roped off called "Hell" – where all rebellious souls are sent? Does this place have simulated fires of varying degrees to punish the victim more or less according to the degree of his or her rebellion? The bombs are getting bigger!

No, you say. Hell is a place where there isn't God. Your punishment will be to never know God. Is that to say that God can be known by some and not by others? And who decides the needed capacity for understanding?

Are souls who obey blessed with a greater capacity and those who don't damned with the original gift? That's interesting. Is that to say that happiness is directly proportional to the capacity for understanding? Is that to say that God holds back on those punished?

How about the idea that God is restricted in His own home? Is not all the world, God's home? How, then, can He consider one portion unworthy of His presence, call it "Hell," and never visit that place of damnation? How, then, can Hell exist as a place where God is not? Or does He exist everywhere and Hell is only not being able to see Him where He is? Are the obedient fitted with some special glasses and the disobedient left without? Give the prophets of this idea some time and I'm sure they will manufacture some special glasses. Once an objection is raised, they will deliver an answer. It may not be smart, but it will be an answer.

Of all the concepts ever proposed as an explanation for the soul, the most unlikely is this one that the soul is directly created by God; yet it is probably the most widely believed. A simple analysis of this concept is to destroy it as one without guts or one having absolutely no chance for being true. How many mind bombs did we explode by following its trail? How many more have been left unexploded?

Those who believe it might say that the unbeliever can think of a thousand reasons to deny it, but a real believer needs only one reason to embrace it – the love of God. God's love is so terrific that it can resolve even the grossest of fates. Can this possibly be true? Or is the correct response one that says it's not the love of

God that creates divine fate for souls, but rather the ignorance of man who knows neither himself nor God and tries to define both within the boundaries of that ignorance?

4

The Soul as Reincarnated

Again, we begin where all theories should begin. When did I begin? Many reincarnationists believe that originally the soul is created by God and then that soul strays from its origin, perhaps by getting lost in the world of flesh. For some reason, the reincarnationists who believe that man has strayed from God somehow believe that the world of the flesh is below God. Now, how a soul could have "descended" into the flesh in the first place is beyond me, but some think this way. Getting away from the flesh that traps a soul seems to be the whole course of a soul that has somehow dropped away from God. It makes no sense to me. Why would a soul consider travel in the flesh useful if the flesh is lacking in God? Why would I want to incarnate – or go into the flesh – if by incarnating, I'm trying to get back to God? If the flesh is somehow distant from God because God is Spirit, why would a soul delve into that which is distant from God in order to get back to God? Those who think that way confuse the jeebers out of me.

Many reincarnationists believe that the soul can wander away from an original perfection in that they can stray from God. God is then limited to some mysterious center, outside of which He doesn't exist. My idea of God is that it is that force or entity that exists everywhere. That is the very definition of God. So, how can there be some so called "center" where God exists and some "outside the center" where God can't exist? With just a little thinking, we can resolve that it cannot be that any being can "stray from God." It can't be so because God must be everywhere. There can be no straying from something that is everywhere.

In truth, then, God cannot be some mystical center from which everything evolves and from which straying occurs. The reincarnationists who see God as creator of souls who can stray from the creator overlook the fact that it is impossible for a soul to stray from God because God is everywhere and cannot be escaped. The soul, then, needs no journey to get back to God; for it could have never left Him – or It.

Another variation of the theory of reincarnation has the soul being the product of some so called, "Big Bang." This theory, too, reaches for the implausible as an answer for the beginning of a soul. It has it own serious field of mind bombs.

What causes this big bang that allegedly allows for the projection of myriads of souls from some mystical and ethereal star of soul energy? What causes this source of energy to explode in the first place? Does it have a place in the universe, like a planet of potential soul energy? It seems to me that this theory has no base in reality and is as much purely speculative as the direct creation by God theory. In short, it offers few answers while it poses multiple questions for which there are no plausible answers.

The "Big Bang" theory, I think, is solely the product of scientists pondering the beginning of the universe. As it is speculated that the universe originated from some cosmic star that exploded, so also it is speculated that souls proceed into existence in the same manner. The cosmic soul star, having all that bounded soul energy, explodes and scatters souls hither and thither. I suppose each soul wanders for a time until it can find a host to take or inspire; and when it does, it turns into a leach sucking experiences from the host body, experiences that serve as fuel for its journey back to the original source.

This is the stuff science fiction is made of, but hardly something a serious soul can consider as plausible. If the original soul pocket exploded and scattered souls from its midst, there would be no parent host to return to. So, where would such a projected journey back to a nonexistent center end? It would seem that the souls coming from this original explosion are doomed to wander forever, unless the journey itself is deemed the essence of the experience. If that is the case, the trip back translates only into a trip without an end.

At least my friend, Emmett, had an end in view within his belief of illusionary soul. He had an end called "oblivion." This particular view of reincarnation projects no end, but rather endless wandering in and out of bodies looking for a parent that has ceased to exist. For all its lacking of plausibility, however, the "Big Bang" theory at least resolves God from judging souls and does not "finitize" God by having Him (or It) be the source of the big bang. If it did, God would have been exploded into a jillion little godlings with the original God being remanded to oblivion. God can't explode and be scattered where He was not; for again, as infinite, God must already exist everywhere. The soul cannot be explained at the expense of dividing or limiting God.

All traditional reincarnationists believe in the sanctity of experience. A soul must experience this or that to be brought into some mystical original alignment with perfection. For reincarnationists, at least for many of them, perfection cannot be found in a current state of being. Like the souls of direct creation by God, most reincarnated souls have to go, or think they have to go, someplace else to find perfection. Over the rise, there may be perfection; but perfection is never at hand; or else the journey will have ended.

But what is this mystical perfection for which they reach? There is always a higher and lower echelon of virtue where ultimate virtue is perfection. That which is low is that which is evil, although evil in a relative sense; and that which is high is that which is good, and perhaps, God Himself.

A major pitfall of most theories of reincarnation is the basic perception that perfection is never at hand and always beyond. Many reincarnationists fail to see that by definition God has to be everywhere at every moment; and therefore, perfection must always be at hand and never out of reach if attainment of God is indeed the definition of perfection.

So what if attainment of God is not the perfection for which they seek? Say that they realize that the deposit to the God-attainment account is already at its maximum. What then? What becomes their objective? Which goal are they seeking by thinking that they have to be born and reborn until they get it right? Many reincarnationists say they have to be recycled, as it were, again and again until they get it right. If attainment of God has already been achieved in spite of themselves, what is the "right" they seek? What do they have to do to get it right?

Is it truth? Will the truth really free them? And if so, for what? Many reincarnationists remind me of travelers who set out for some far land without having any idea how far it is. "Getting it right" translates to reaching the unknown destiny. It could be a hundred miles, a thousand, a million, a trillion, a zillion. They keep trudging along because stopping and recognizing their destiny has already been achieved is not part of the plan.

Another concept that many reincarnationists love is the concept of realms or strata or dimensions or planes. The soul must penetrate some imaginary plane of existence to reach into the alleged dimension beyond. It's like the imaginary dimension beyond belongs to a different intensity of energy. It's a whole new world.

I think this perception results as a logical conclusion of the soul travel idea. If souls travel, they must travel someplace and toward some goal of aspiration.

So imaginary planes of existence that divide those who might fail from those who might succeed are injected into the scheme of things.

From there, we have wise souls who have penetrated the planes speaking to those who need to penetrate them. Souls speak claiming experience in a different plane; and students of reincarnation gather to hear the "all wise one." But are those wise souls any different than the prophets of the direct creation corral? Am I to believe that planes of existence do exist because some philanthropic soul "on the other side" claims as much? This wise one would naturally tell me what I want to hear since he is at hand to do the telling in the first place, rather than pursuing his own adventure.

What else can he or she say? Would you expect him to say: *I speak to you from the same plane. The only difference is that you have a body and I do not. You are as I, no better, no worse. You have no where to go but where you are.* Would he or she likely get my attention by stating equality?

I think many of the so called "wise ones" who seek channels through which to speak are souls searching for attention, much like preachers willing to give advise. A preacher needs an audience; and so does a "wise one" from the other side. It stands to reason there must be souls living in the beyond who need attention because there are many living in mortality who do. Are attention seeking souls really going to stop their practices when they pass into the great beyond? I don't think so.

So, what is it that a great wise one, like a great prophet, can tell me that I don't already know or have a way of knowing? Is the place they are more miraculous than the place I am? Not if God is equally here and there. Are they in less physical pain and suffering than I? Probably because if they are in a beyond, they are without bodies that allow pain; but when I pass, too, into that great beyond, I will be as they; and all their accumulated wisdom will not have affected the achievement.

5

The Soul as Generated By a Natural Soul

(*The Parent Soul Concept*)

So, here we are, totally suspicious of the soul as a direct creation of God and the soul as reincarnated – and even the soul as an entity that dies with the body. Have we not covered all bases?

No – we haven't. There is another I'd like to suggest. The soul does not originate as a direct creation of a personal God, nor as a starlet of a soulful energy exploding from a big bang. It exists, not so mysteriously at all, as the progeny of another soul. We have been looking too high for the answer; and the answer is only navel deep, as it were. Look into your belly button and there is the answer.

You see, we really do not have to know the process to understand that it is so because like all processes in Nature, none of which we thoroughly know, the birth of the soul must only be a reflection of Nature's other processes. After all, the soul is natural. Is it not? It must, then, have a natural explanation, not a supernatural one; and it must have an explanation that is ongoing that takes place on a consistent basis like all other processes in Nature. We're not looking for an answer that is a once in a million years happening. Rather, we should be looking for an answer that is happening now.

There are many, I know, who would resist this notion that the soul is natural, as natural as the body. These are the ones who want to see God in Heaven and not in Hell. These are the ones who want to see God in a church or in a prophet and not in a kitchen. These are the ones who want to see God in the priest and not in the prostitute. These are the ones who divide reality into regions of good and evil and separate the miracle from the miraculous.

Why not answer the soul with a natural explanation? Why go beyond, unless one sees Nature somehow as less worthy of virtue than the God Which creates it? If the soul exists at all as an individual entity that is not dependent upon the body for its life, why should the soul not have to follow the same rules as everything else in Nature?

And what are the rules? We just have to look at the rest of Nature to find the answer. In all of the rest of Nature, anything that exists as a living being comes from something else and comes from something that is like it. This is the evidence we have somehow totally ignored when discussing the soul.

I began my own personal existence at birth on December 3rd, 1941. Everything else that began on that date came from something else and came from something that is like it. Why should my soul have been different? Why should it, too, not have had its birth from another born earlier - given that my soul is a living entity, independent of my body?

We're talking independent entity here, not dependent entity like my friend, Emmett's, illusive soul. Given that my soul is an independent entity, why should it not have to follow the same rules of all other independent living entities of Nature? That is the way of Nature; and it is foolish of me to think I am different; for in both body and soul, I believe I am a son of Nature.

Now, perhaps my soul was not born at the same time my body was born. Perhaps it was born at the same time as my conception or when my gender evolved within my mother's womb at six weeks or nine weeks or whenever, but at some point, even if before my conception as a body, my soul was probably born of another soul. It was never born of God as a consequent of a direct creation. That is not to say that God is not in me. It's only to say that God did not do me personally; and He or She or It did not do you personally either.

That's a tough one for a lot of folks to swallow. They so want a personal relationship with God and need the same. So, an impersonal participation of God in the birth of a soul is totally unacceptable. The Jews of old, and even today, believed so strong that a personal relationship with a stern God figure is needed that they fomented the dogma of the messiah, a masculine Godly figure, to fulfill it. The Christians then took the same dogma and brought God into a personal mode in the character of Jesus. The need for a personal relationship with God is deep – very, very deep.

If there was evidence in reality that the body is "poof created" by God, then I would have reason to believe that the soul is also "poof created." But there is no evidence of the body being a poof or instant creation of God. Accordingly, there is no reason to believe that the soul is either. If the soul is not the product of an instantaneous personal creation, then, it must be the product of an ever consistent natural process of generation.

Through the wonderful power of observation, two principles of natural generation are obvious. **Number one, all things that exist in Nature come from something else – not themselves; and number two, all things that exist in Nature come from something that is like them.** We may not understand why it has to be that way, but it should be obvious to the most casual observer that it is that way.

It is obvious, for instance, that a cat - or a body of a cat - can't come from a dog. It just doesn't happen that way. It's obvious, too, that a fish can't come from a lion, nor a bird from a bear, nor a human from a cow. The plain simple truth is that in every ongoing process in Nature, without exception, all things are born of something else and are born of something that is like them.

Given, then, that the soul even qualifies as an independent entity that perhaps can marry with a body, it, too, should have to follow the rules of all generation. It must come from its own kind, which is to say, it must come from another soul or souls. The power of observation, the greatest tool of wisdom, will tell us that.

Of course, we can deny our observation and claim that the soul does not have to follow the rules of all other generation. We surely can do that – and have done it and continue to do it. We can cling to a notion not enforced by any observation that some things in existence can be created instantaneously. Nothing in Nature is created outside of natural generation out of thin air. It just doesn't happen that way. Does it? Why should the soul be different? **Why shouldn't the two principles of all natural generation have to apply to the soul as well?** Like everything else, the soul, if it exists at all as an independent entity, must come from something else and must come from something that is like it.

Observation, then, can tell us all we need to know about the soul. We need no special laboratory, nor prophet, nor ethereal wise man. We need only to observe and to pay attention to the general rules of all generation. **Know the rules – then apply them.** That's all we have to do. It's really not all that difficult, unless we make it so; and knowing the rules and applying them doesn't detract from the mystery of God in it all either. It only redefines it a little. The fantastic mysteries of God can never be challenged by any degree of knowledge of humankind, even as humankind comes to understand more about itself.

6

Issues

The Natural Soul Concept

Resolves

I believe the *"Natural Soul Concept"* resolves a lot of issues that other theories do not, although it doesn't answer everything. Just for the heck of it, though, let me offer a few issues that I think the Natural Soul Concept resolves. How about – seven? OK?

<u>Number one</u>, it absolves God from having to be finite because the idea does not require a personal God. Personal is finite because personal is limiting or defined by a relationship. Where there is a relationship, there is definition. God, as infinite, cannot be "defined" or stated to be here and not there. This is important because we get ourselves into a lot of confusion trying to bring God down to our level to satisfy the need for a personal God. To create man or to judge him or to personally

bless him, God has been personalized to get the job done. He has been "finitized" or limited by virtue of the process imposed upon Him.

We can't have it both ways. We can't have both an infinite God and a finite God; and we can't make God into something He (or She or It) is not just to satisfy a need to make God the leading character of a fairy tale. It's not like we are excluding God from the picture. We are only recognizing there is no place in the picture He is not. The Natural Soul Concept doesn't need a personalized God. Therefore, it does not need soul creation, soul judgment, or soul blessing by a personal God. The blessing is reality.

God is not finite. God is infinite. That means that God is everywhere. God is therefore in us, not out of us as if we are external carvings of a Divine Sculptor. **We are not external carvings. We are internal expressions.** We can't be outside of God because God cannot be outside of us. The Natural Soul Concept resolves the issue of the ages that would have God being outside of all that God is creating. To be only outside of me is to be limited. To be only inside of me is to be limited – or finite. God is not limited. God is both inside and outside of me and you. God is infinite – not finite!

**Number two, the Natural Soul Concept provides an answer for the beginning of a soul.** The other theories suggest notions that are more speculations and impositions than answers. You can't even begin to verify them. They remain pure guesses. The Natural Soul Concept, however, offers an answer that is consistent with a Nature of answers. Nature does all beginnings in the same way. All living things come from other living things and come from living things that are like them.

Is my soul, a finite entity if it exists at all, like God? How, then, could it have been issued from God in a personal way? Is my soul like a ray of light? Is any living thing like a ray of light? How, then, could my soul be the son of a beam of light? We could go on, but there's no need.

At one time in his history, man was convinced that his body came from a deity too, but science has come to offer a rational explanation for the process of physical generation. If the soul does exist as an independent entity, most likely, it also respects some natural law of origin. Consistency of mind would demand it. It is unreasonable to assume that Nature has one rule for one set of life and another rule for another set. Most likely, all life attends to the same rule of origin – or rules of origin.

What is the soul? The Natural Soul explanation can't answer that with certainty any more than any of the other theories can, but if I were to have to define it, personally this would be my answer: *The soul is an individual expression that resides in time and place which records for posterity the experiences of life.* But individual expressions have beginnings. In my opinion, the Natural Soul Concept offers a far better explanation for the beginning of a soul than does any other theory about the soul.

Regardless of its origin, however, I think it is important to realize that whatever the soul is, it is an individual. That means it can be owned – as it can own. As something that can be owned, ideally we should own our own souls. Too many souls are individuals owned not by themselves, but by others who wish to control them and make them their subjects. Whatever the soul is, it should be your own as my soul should be my own. I may have come from another, but once given birth, I should belong first to me. That is not to say I can't belong to others as well, but if I do not belong first to me, then as far as I am concerned, I am a soul without dignity for having to depend upon another for meaning. The soul is no different that anything else in creation. As completely filled with God, it should need nothing outside of itself for a sense of completion; and any soul that thinks it needs another to be fulfilled lacks esteem for its own perfection.

**Number three**, the Natural Soul Concept provides an answer for the ending of the soul – or the destiny of the soul or a soul. If the soul ages, it will probably also die, but who is to say that it does age? Assuming, however, that it does age, lots would worry about the prospect of a soul dying. They don't want their souls to die, but wishing against it won't make it so if that is the end of the process.

Do all things in Nature die? All that we can see, yes; but keep in mind, there's a lot we can't see. Maybe the soul will die and maybe it won't, but regardless of any aging process, it is likely that the soul continues after the death of the body for some indefinite period of time. How else could it become a parent soul itself? Then, too, maybe the soul is exempt from breaking down or aging and therefore is trapped in existence. Who knows? I don't. But knowing it or not knowing it won't alter the process, whatever that process is. The wise man will just let Nature take its own course and be grateful for the participation.

__Number four__, the Parent or Natural Soul Concept provides a much needed answer for the tradition of a soul. Why is one soul naturally angry and another always at peace while both souls enjoy the same benefits? The Natural Soul Concept would say that souls, like bodies, naturally inherit characteristics and moods, and maybe even memories, of the parent soul. Though a soul may not have lived incarnated in a previous life, it would be as if it did because it will inherit the experiences of the parent soul which did live before.

It is also possible, if not probable, that a parent soul would stick around its child and provide some degree of providence or protection or guidance. Maybe the presence you sometimes feel that gives you a warm feeling of being loved and cherished doesn't come from a personal God, but rather from a personal soul from your own soulful tradition, be it your own parent soul or souls or just a relative soul or friend. The possibilities of a soulful providence are endless, given that you are the son or daughter of another soul or of other souls.

The Natural Soul explanation provides grounding for a soul like none of the other theories do. My soul is grounded to a parent soul, and, as such, can reasonably expect some degree of "angelic" assistance; however, it's also possible that some soulful parents, like some human parents, will not choose to stick around and will, in fact, abandon their progeny soul or souls.

It would seem likely, too, that a soul, when it has finished its journey in mortality, will join and be joined by the tradition of souls that preceded it. Death for some of us may mean quite a homecoming; and for others of us, it may be a solo. Life is like that – and probably so is death or life beyond death.

Connected with this discussion of the tradition or heritage of a soul, the Natural Soul Concept explains the possibility of soul mates – and even soul twins. Who's to say that a parent soul can't make twins and who's to say those twins can't decide to incarnate at the same time? Even if the positioning was at opposite ends of a culture, each of the twins would likely be initially disposed with the same character traits – and consequently, may have the same likes and dislikes.

If the soul also influences physical development, the bodies of those two separated souls could also develop along the same pattern, depending upon the blueprint or soul map inherited from the same parent soul. I'd say that's an interesting possibility; and the Natural Soul Theory would say it is plausible.

The issue of soul mates could be similar. There could be another very similar to me in the world as a brother or sister from the same parent. It would be no wonder that two souls could be attracted as if one entity because their heritage may have paved the way to that end. The Natural Soul Theory would provide a very sensible answer to the issue of soul mates. Some of us may have multiple soul mates in the world. Perhaps it is our destiny to find and even marry with one another.

Also connected with this discussion of the tradition of a soul under the tutorship of a parent soul, homosexuality could find an explanation. Say that a given heritage of souls has been male for successive generations, or has selected masculine forms as hosts; and then a male inclined heritage with a natural attraction to females decides to go with a female progeny – or a feminine form. What might be a possible result? The tradition and blueprint of that soul could have been so paved with attraction to the female sex that the current progeny keeps the same tradition and attraction. Thus, the daughter could find herself attracted only to other females. It's a thought. It might be hard to alter a habit in one generation.

While on this subject of body selection, it might be worthwhile to consider the issue of deformity and poverty selection here. If we are right on this matter that souls select bodies, and maybe even control their development, why would a soul intentionally choose to go with the unattractive – like deformity and poverty? Perhaps the answer is to correct an imbalance by a soul intent on altering itself for its own tradition.

Maybe a tradition of souls has a habit of kicking dogs – and a rebel soul decides it's time to stop kicking dogs. So it becomes one to correct the imbalance. Instead of being one to kick dogs, it becomes a kicked dog. Or maybe a tradition of souls has a habit of sneering at the poor – and a rebel soul decides it's time to stop sneering. So it becomes one of the sneered poor. Or maybe a tradition of souls has a habit of deforming and demeaning other persons – and a rebel soul decides it's time to stop deforming and demeaning. So it becomes one of the deformed so as to embrace them.

Oh, what wonderful mysteries lie in the selections of a soul! It may seem this line of thinking is crazy, but I don't think it's crazy at all. The world of souls must be like the world of people because souls become people. As there will always be rebel people from human traditions, it follows that there will always be rebel souls from soulful traditions. Rebellion often takes the form of choosing the opposite of a disliked tradition. So why not for souls too?

If my tradition is one of abusing and I decide I don't want to continue the tradition, the best possible approach could be to go over to the abused side so as to see things from there. That way, in a rather dramatic fashion, I could correct the imbalance caused by my tradition and right things so as to proceed along my own very different course.

What I mean to say from this conjecture about imbalance is that, though a soul would naturally have a tradition to uphold, it could, if it wanted, change course. It could go from an inclination to be rich to an inclination to be poor just to change an undesired course. Again, the reason for saying so is that humans do it sometimes – and souls are only inhuman entities before they become human entities or human souls.

On the other hand, however, a soul could choose the tradition of its soulful family only because it lacked the need or desire to change a family course. Thus, one of a tradition of poverty could choose it again; and one of a tradition of riches could choose that again; and one of a tradition of moderation could choose that again too.

It could be, then, that a rebel soul is personally taking charge to change its destiny from its tradition when embracing an attitude and a practice different from its tradition. But consider this too. Say that an entire tradition is desiring a change and decides to give birth to a soul to represent that desired change. That progeny, then, would be *"sent into the world with a mission,"* but that mission would be for the entire tradition, not just for itself.

In such a case, and it's reasonable to expect that such a scheme could happen because it also happens in mortal mode, a progeny soul would carry the load of an entire tradition. It would be like that soul, in doing battle with an entire world, would be doing battle for an entire soulful family or community or tradition.

On the other hand, the representation need not be a rebellious one from the manner of the parent tradition. It could well be that a soul is continuing an age old tradition by sending a son or a daughter into the world to do this or that. Through that progeny, an entire tradition could, in a sense, be living and maturing and caring or hating or killing and raping, whatever the case may be. In this light, too, I am sure there are myriads of cases that are entirely reflective of this kind of setting.

For instance, could Christ have been a disciple for his tradition? Could it have been literally true that he was *"sent into the world by his father"*? Personally, I think the chances are extremely slim that he did not fit this mold of mission.

And what was his mission? It's hard to be certain about that because there is so much confusion and contradiction in the Gospels about his possible mission. In one case, we find him representing a tradition out to judge the world and condemn it for non-belief; and in another reflection, we have him representing a tradition intent on telling the world that Heaven is at hand and that Heaven is for everyone who recognizes that the world is the blessing of God and not a trap for the soul.

As so often happens, writers and reporters report what they see – and that may not be truly reflective of reality. Matthew, Mark, Luke, and John speculated in their own vague ways about the mission of Christ, but each of them told of it as supportive of their own particular view of life. In other words, they fit Christ to their belief. They didn't change their belief to fit Christ because they did not know the real Christ; or, at least, such is my opinion. I think they represented an earthly tradition which required a messiah; and in Christ, they found one – or made one. They represented a tradition that saw sin as a human inheritance that could only be washed away by a sinless God; and then they made a god of Christ to wash away that sin. What else could they do – given their perception of life – remain lost forever?

Who was Christ and what was his mission? That's anybody's guess, as it was also the guesses of Matthew, Mark, Luke, John – and Peter, who may have driven them all. Each of these reporters had an axe to grind with their renditions of Christ. And what is the real story? Well, I guess it's written in the wind and in the Holy Book of the soulful tradition and family of Christ; and perhaps that will not be found in any book here on Earth.

Even as I say that, however, I do believe there is a version of Christ that comes much closer to the real person than that offered by any of the favored Gospels of the *BIBLE*. In 1945 in a cave in Egypt, there was found an ancient script that has since been related as *THE GOSPEL ACCORDING TO THOMAS*. By carbon dating, it has been determined that this script, written in an Egyptian verse called Coptic, has been in that cave off the Nile River since the 4th Century A.D. I do not choose to offer a personal interpretation of that work here, but I think it's worth noting that I have offered an interpretation of that work in a work of my own that I call *JESUS VIA THOMAS COMMENTARIES*. The Christ that I found in the work by Thomas, alleged to be Thomas, one of the Apostles of Christ, is a very different Christ than that presented in the regular Gospels. At least, I think so. It is worth while to note that here, I think; but having noted it, let me proceed.

NOTE: In 2012, I started a writings website that is intended to include all of my writings to that point - from 1963 - 2012. One of the features of that website is called *OUT IN THE OPEN* - Volumes 1 through 8 - with each volume representing a chronological period of my writings. Volume 7 of that *OUT IN THE OPEN* feature includes works written in 2009. In that year, I wrote my *JESUS VIA THOMAS COMMENTARIES* - as well as interpretations of *THE GOSPEL OF MARY MAGDALENE.* I call my Gospel of Mary interpretative work by the name of *JESUS VIA MARY COMMENTARIES.* If interested in either of those efforts, simply go to my writings website - www.una-bella-vita.com - and tap into Volume 7 of the *OUT IN THE OPEN* feature. OK? Keep in mind, however, that my interpretations are my own. So, like any set of interpretations, take them as personal opinions only.

Thanks! FWB - 5/7/2015

Number five, the Natural Soul Concept provides an answer concerning the judgment of souls. God may not judge souls, lest He or She or It be "finitized" in the process; but that does not mean there is no judgment. The old saying, **What goes around, comes around,** says it all. There is no forgiveness for hurting and being hurt except by stopping the action that's doing it. The Natural Soul Concept absolves God of judgment, but it places judgment squarely where it belongs – on the individual of judgment.

If I am a kind soul, in mortal life or hereafter, it is reasonable to assume I will continue the kindness. If I am a mean soul, I will continue the meanness. If I am a joyful soul, the joy will continue. If I am a pessimistic soul, the pessimism will continue. If I am an optimistic soul, the optimism will continue. *Continuation of a state of mind is the main judgment of a soul.*

There are many who don't like that prospect. How dare it be so that a man who murders another should not be punished for the deed! It may seem otherwise, but they are punished by continuing their state of mind and not having an easy way to escape it. Isn't that punishment enough?

Those who answered "No" are likely subject to their own judgment to continue their state of mind of mercilessness. I don't think it would be much better to be a man with a merciless state of mind than it would be to be a man with a mean state of mind. In fact, there is not much difference between the two. In effect, meanness and mercilessness are similar states of mind. So if you are all so concerned that the mean person is not getting his due, perhaps you should be looking to change your ways because your own mean heart is lurching there close behind your revengeful attitude. Meanness and mercilessness are more like siblings than opposites because both are conducted by angry souls. The Natural Soul Concept would say that judgment is automatic, self-imposed by attitude, and universal. No one can escape it because no one can escape themselves. Can they?

This thing about it not being easy to change ones state of mind should not be underestimated. Perhaps that's why we are born into bodies in the first place, to change a state of mind – given that a soul is a guest of a body host. Why would a soul choose to fill or inform a body if not for some advantage a body could provide that a bodiless existence could not? Maybe bodies, through sensation, allow change within a soul by some soulful feedback. Maybe they can't alter their state of mind outside of an atmosphere of change that doesn't exist in purely soulful existence.

If so, how about this? A soul might yearn for freedom from the body because life is seen as a burden rather than as a joyful experience, then is freed from the body through death, and then has to continue its state of mind of feeling life is a burden without ability to change or correct the state of mind without being born again. That's what you could call a vicious circle; and that's also judgment. It's like being caught in a spiral that repeats and repeats and repeats. So the wise man will not take judgment lightly.

Then, too, there may be the judgment of revenge to consider, perhaps as heartless and determined as the injury we imposed in our turn. We are free of a vengeful God for sure because God is inside of us and not outside of us to be able to be vengeful, but we may not be free of vengeful souls out to get even. Is it not likely that if I should bind others against their will, when they are freed – even if by death itself – they may choose to try and bind me against my will? That is if they are revenge minded and cannot let that go because they are caught up in a judgment of their own desired revenge.

Given that souls might have an ability to track or track down other souls, revenge would likely be predictable as a judgment upon a soul guilty of inflicting pain or death in his turn simply because of the vengeful character of many souls. Of the six million Jews executed under Adolph Hitler, for instance, maybe one million of those may be revenge minded. How would you like to be pursued by a million militants and their families? That may well become the "eternal" fate of an Adolph Hitler. How would you like to be marked for death upon birth? That could be a consequence of the judgment of revenge.

NOTE: If I am correct about one like Hitler being the subject of revenge in subsequent lives, I think it worthwhile to recognize that Hitler would likely be a subject - or object - of revenge only as long as he - or she or it in a next life - maintained a "persecutorial complex." It is that state of mind that would make Hitler a "permanent" prey for those who are revenge minded. Anger attracts anger. Hate attracts hate. If Hitler maintained an attitude of hate - as might be probable - then Hitler could be subject to lots of revenge minded folks; however, if Hitler were to change and become "kindness oriented," then he would probably drop off the radar of revenge - or hate - minded souls in a subsequent

life. That, of course, might be difficult because of the nature of judgment itself that we probably continue as we were; but it's good to keep in mind that it is likely that a change of heart - or soul - is always possible. In that light, "redemption," if you want to call it that, is always possible. No one need fear having to endure a "permanent hell."

Thanks! FWB - 5/8/2015

Number six, the Natural Soul theory provides an answer for the prevailing existence of churches in the world. Why are there so many religions, all claiming to represent the one true God? Is not that God the same for all? Why, then, all the different churches, each one disclaiming the validity of the other for this reason or that? The answer is, it's probably different soulful traditions allowing for their own control of things.

Would it not stand to reason that if my state of mind is to control others, especially their souls, that I would want to establish some structure for that purpose? Presto, a church, at least the kind that seeks to regulate and not simply, suggest. I'm sure there are some souls, like there are some humans, whose desired state of mind is to gather souls. After all, I suppose souls need company too. On the part of some, I'm sure there is a continuous effort to add to the fold. A church might be a proper vehicle to that end.

This is not to say that churches are of no value. Certainly not. In his own way, Christ came to add to his fold and declare his church for doing that. I am sure there are many Christian churches which actually reflect the actual aims and intentions of the real Christ; but there are also many churches which have no idea about the real Christ but think they do and generously use the name of Christ to gain adherents to their own faiths. This is not to argue for or against any particular church. It's just to argue that the Natural Soul Concept offers an answer as to why there are churches and so many of them.

And finally, *__Number seven__, the Natural Soul Concept and theory and explanation offers us a reason, a tremendously motivating one, to go free.* The greatest bondage is ignorance. That is, the greatest cause of bondage is ignorance. To the degree that we allow ourselves to be herded into some soul corral or other, we will have always been ignorant to that same degree. We are capable of controlling our own destiny – or of being controlled by another's destiny.

We can establish our own soulful traditions and then bare our children souls within the constraints of that tradition. We are free to have fun, if that's what we want; and, unfortunately, we are also free to impede others from having their kind of fun and fulfillment. If we do choose the way of impeding others, however, then one judgment we will suffer will be the loss of our own freedom. The wise soul knows that it is impossible to impose without being imposed upon. **To restrict another is to be restricted by virtue of our expenditure of energy; for if we restrict others, we are not free to** be free of them. In making others our prisoners, they become our responsibilities as we become their servants. Indeed, judgment may wear mysterious robes.

We are free of a God Who or Which commands not to eat of the apples of the orchard. We are free to enjoy the meal of our own choosing, keeping in mind that dietary habits and all other habits are ours for the making, but also ours for the keeping. It's a terribly old cliché, but the Natural Soul Idea would agree all the way: *We can make the bed we want, but we also have to lie in the bed we make.* Life and Judgment are strictly up to us.

7

Reincarnation

and

The Natural Soul Concept

Perhaps there is not one single answer in respect to the total life of a soul. If you will, let us consider a marriage of concepts. *Perhaps the proper marriage is one between the Parent Soul or Natural Soul Concept and Reincarnation.* Given that the beginning of a soul is not a direct creation by God in a personal sense and not from some cataclysmic explosion of some magical soul star, it would seem feasible that a born soul might choose to reincarnate indefinitely.

Who's to say that a soul can't do this? Who knows the mechanics of incarnation to say it can't be so? I know of no one. How about you? *It would seem to me very logical that if a soul could incarnate once, it could do so forever – given that it is truly or practically immortal and given that the soul controls the process.*

If, however, souls are infused into bodies as part of the process of physical generation, reincarnation is not likely. If somehow the birth of a soul is intertwined with a greater process of life and conception and embryonic development, it is not likely that an existent soul could play a part in the drama.

Perhaps a parent soul wanting to give birth to a son or daughter uses a human conception, or any animal conception for that matter, as a cocoon in which to nestle the child soul. If so, this would imply that the entry of a soul into a carnal form would be a one time event. Perhaps birth of soul in some crazy way depends on physical generation and can't happen outside of it. If so, then, it is unlikely souls can be reborn within a subsequent conception; for there would be no need. I suppose it would be possible, though, that a soul could choose the generation of carnal life as the time to repeat itself in a child or children souls. Accordingly, maybe a parent soul, as such, would never reincarnate and any soul would only incarnate once – as it is given birth by a parent soul. It does make for some very interesting speculation. Doesn't it?

If, however, a soul is already born before the incarnation takes place, and was born itself outside of the process of incarnation, having a life totally independent of the flesh, then there is no reason why the incarnation process can't be repeated indefinitely for any given soul. Given the apparent comings and goings of souls in some cases of human experience, the evidence strongly suggests the latter process to be the right one. Souls are already born before they take possession of bodies. They may not be born as part of the process of incarnation itself.

Assuming reincarnation as real, however, what is the evidence to suggest that existing entities take possession of bodies? Perhaps it can best be illustrated in cases of so called "possession" where a human person is visited by another soul who takes charge or tries to take charge and take control away from the resident soul. This could explain schizophrenia and multiple personalities. There may be multiple souls trying to occupy the same body. Normally, the result would have to be confusion and conflict with souls fighting each other for control, unless the multiple possession is by kindred souls.

Then there is the evidence of "obsession" that would suggest the existence of souls before incarnation takes place. There are many instances where external souls, or some external phenomena, have attempted to interrupt a life or a situation or even attack a person with whatever force it is that bodiless souls have. Some would dismiss activities due to obsession as hallucination on the part of the recipient, but it is clearly possible that visits and involvements on the part of foreign souls, friendly and otherwise, could occur if it is so that a resident soul visited a body initially. If one soul can visit a body, perhaps multiple souls can visit that same body.

The possibilities are there; and they are very real. So called "devils" could be nothing more than antagonistic souls intervening to try and upset or control a resident soul. I'm sure this happens continuously within the many dramas of life. We've all heard of voices commanding a soul to do this or that. Sometimes what is commanded is friendly; and sometimes it is not. I suppose the kind of command would depend entirely upon the nature or character of the one giving the command.

Perhaps our asylums are filled with people who are victims of possession, and even obsession. If there are multiple masters of opposing minds trying to control one body host, only chaos could result; and this might be the chaos reflected in much insanity.

As suggested, however, multiple possession need not be antagonistic, although I doubt that much friendly possession occurs because of a respect of friendly souls for one another. Friends do not normally invade one another. Friendly multiple possession probably doesn't occur, but friendly visits and even friendly assistance in ways unknown by the resident soul probably occur all the time. Maybe that would explain inexplicable powers that some people feel sometime. Maybe there's a kindred soul around offering a boost to a friend.

Anyway, back to the possibility of incarnation happening at the agency of an existent soul and not a soul being born as a soul, multiple possession is perhaps our best evidence that souls do, in fact, exist to take possession of a body – whether that be a baby body or otherwise. If it can happen to an adult person, it could certainly happen to a baby. From that, I think reincarnation is far more fact than fiction.

Why would souls reincarnate? That's the big question. Isn't it? I suggested in a previous Part that perhaps the key is the sensation of the animal form, allowing change to be reflected in a hosted soul. Maybe this is the answer and maybe not. I don't think things happen or can happen for no reason. So, it's obvious to me that the flesh must provide some advantage to a soul occupying a body or else it wouldn't incarnate in the first place.

What would our reason tell us about the advantages of the flesh to a soul? Well, for what it's worth, I've thought about that and it seems to me the motives, though many, can be reduced to several simple ones – **to ride, to hide, to find, and to deride.**

It may seem strange, and even contradictory at times, but I suspect some souls marry with bodies to **hide** in them for various reasons. Some marry with bodies to **find** the truths of reality. Some only want to use them for a **ride.** And, unfortunately, there are some whose only mission is to **deride** and control others.

I have known lots of people in this world who care nothing at all for the truth. It's meaningless to them. Their only interest is to ride the waves, to use the world for the moment, to want or to make a fortune, and to be comfortable. A soul born into the world to seek adventure for only the sake of adventure is a rider. These would use the flesh only for the sake of comfort and adventure and fun and thrills and would resist any attempt to defeat that goal. Generally speaking, among – but not restricted to - this crowd of souls, we would have persons intent on realizing a fortune – of their own making or not.

As I have known lots of rider souls, I have also known lots of hider souls. These are the ones who don't want the truth and hide in the flesh to avoid it. Perhaps the last place you will find a hider is in a nudist community. That would be like trying to escape your shadow by running in the sun. Hider souls do not care for the light that much. They prefer the shade and the dark and the freedom to reach for fantasy.

Many hider souls may oppose loose standards because of a fear they would be expected to follow suit. They may not want to follow suit. So, for instance, they may oppose as immoral any attempt to make nakedness and truth exposition acceptable. Hiders are often desperate; and the last thing they want is for someone to show up with a flashlight in the dark. As a defense mechanism, they may well try to ban flashlights.

Then, there is the finder soul – the one who marries with the flesh to find out about the world of reality through it, including the reality of him or herself. The finder soul is interested – first and foremost – in the truth as he or she finds it, not necessarily as another might present it. The finder uses the flesh to observe its truths and its mysteries and its wonders and relates those truths, mysteries, and wonders to its experience as a soul.

Lastly, there is the derider soul – the soul whose only aim for living is to control others in life. This is the one who insists on making the rules and insists that others within his or her circle of experience abide by them. Personally, I do not understand the ones of this mentality. I have no need whatever to control others and have absolutely no sympathy for it. But there are so many in this world who have great desire to control others and subject others as if it is only in the control of others that there is any meaning to their existence. These are the ones who are the complete opposite of my dear, departed friend, Emmett. Like Emmett thrived on being insignificant, the derider souls thrive on a sense of significance.

Of course, some souls would be interested in a little mix of soulful temperaments too. I know I am such a one. The only temperament that I do not personally cherish is the derider sentiment. One moment, I use my body as a mirror and the next I use it as a carrier; but mostly, I think, I use my body and all reality to find the truths of life – even as I also take great pride in using my body to ride the waves of sensation just for the purpose of experiencing the feel of it all. One moment, I may use my body to intently study life and watch it for what it does; and the next, I may be relaxing with a drink in my hand and simply acting like a passenger in love with travel.

It stands to reason that different souls will choose to handle life and the opportunities of life differently since people do. Different souls may have different objectives; and contrary to a lot of oppressive moralists in this world, each soul has its own right to have its own objective – and even the right to change objectives throughout the course of a life.

My own personal objective, for instance, is to find the truth – and maybe tell about it. In fact, that's what this work on the soul is all about – to tell the truth as I have discovered it. The main reason I am writing this essay work is to offer an idea, the idea that souls begin as children of other souls and come together with bodies for the experiences that can be realized within them. As I have struggled in my life with the beginning of the soul and have searched for an answer, I can't help but feel that others want an answer – or answers – too. Maybe my found answer (and answers) isn't for you; but then again, maybe you can find it realistic and rewarding – if it's realism you want.

As for me, it is realism I want. I do not want superficial explanations grounded in fairy tales. I'm not a fairy. I'm a natural human person with a natural soul and a natural body; and I cherish them both. I want realism because only realism can open my eyes to what life is and what I should be as a son of life; but, then, you see, I am one of those finder souls.

Reincarnation seems likely to me because, given a natural beginning of a soul at the outset, the evidence is overwhelming to suggest it. From the evidence of multiple possession to the realism that experience seems to never end, it seems souls exist and are not just figments of our imaginations. *Incarnation by an existing phenomenon that could be called the "soul" seems real; and if incarnation is real, how can reincarnation not be?*

8

Prayer

In my opinion, the expression of a soul is the basic prayer of that soul. We pray according to how we think and how we act. Souls need to pray and do pray with whatever consciousness they represent. Prayer can be vocal or silent, individual or social, solemn or light, spontaneous or formal.

In general, prayer accomplishes two things: *It establishes or confirms a certain perception or consciousness or awareness and it locates each of us for a particular providence.* For those of us who believe that the soul is only an illusion, only the first purpose for prayer could be perceived as valid. For those of us who believe in the soul as an independent entity, both purposes are valid. Oh, I think the second purpose is valid for those who think of the soul as an illusion too because even if they are denying it, they are caught within the boundaries of some providence.

All souls, regardless of belief, pray whether they think they do or not. Every soul, by virtue of being, has to establish or support a particular perception or outlook on life. We have to think of life in one way or another, even if the thought is one of indifference. If so, our prayer is simply one of indifference, but it is a prayer. It's the expression or communication of a soul. Prayer is only the language of the soul; and every soul must speak some language.

Like any other talent, however, prayer can be tuned into an art by focus and attention to it. It's much like music perhaps. In each of us there is a natural rhythm that is music, but only some of us attend to that rhythm and become musicians in the process. Others of us have a song to sing, but never choose to sing it. Our prayer, at best, is an inattentive one – or one without concentration. As my friend, Nancy Remmenga, often says to me: *Don't let death catch you, Frank, with your song unsung!* – or something like that..

To attentively pray is to supply the chords to a song that is already there. To attentively pray is to unify the body with the mind of the soul, to bring them together and let out the sound of a symphony. *The best kind of prayer, I think, is simply listening to the logic dictated by one's soul and obeying the dictation, keeping in mind that soul tunes can be as different and as many as there are souls to sing.*

Prayers can be spoken or thought, depending upon the reason for them. If the reason or purpose is only to speculate on or confirm a perception or awareness, thought is sufficient. If the reason is to locate ourselves for a particular soulful providence, vocalization would likely be useful. Thinking a prayer is much like writing a letter. Vocalizing it is like sending it. Sometimes writing a letter is sufficient, perhaps as needed therapy, but at other times, we need to send it so that another can read it.

Prayer is a way of staying in touch with a preferred presence or providence, which, in essence, is a respective attitude. There are souls out there who are gentle and prefer the way of kindness. If we wish to belong to that family or community of souls and that providence, be it our own specific soul origin or not, praying a prayer of gentleness or kindness and a message of kindness locates us for identification by the community of gentle souls.

On the other hand, there are also souls out there, or probably are, that are mean and prefer the way of meanness. If we wish to belong to that community of souls and that providence or type of providence, praying a prayer of domination and mercilessness and meanness locates us for identification by the community of mean souls – or a community of mean souls. There are probably many communities of mean souls like there are probably many communities of gentle souls. *Support of a given identified soul by its chosen type of providence amounts to the providence of that soul.*

Can a prayer of kindness or gentleness be intercepted by a mean soul or vice versa? It's probably much like a world of many languages or dialects. Should I be a man of strict temperament, insisting on speaking and understanding only English, I would never pay attention to another speaking French. The Frenchman could talk a blue streak right in front of me and I would not understand a word. If he should refuse an understanding of English, we could both live as neighbors and never hear one another.

Prayer, I think, is like that. It can only be received by a familiar temperament and can never be intercepted by a stranger to that temperament. We can pray our prayer, then, and send it out, knowing that only those intended to hear it can hear it and will hear it. That is a very comforting notion, indeed. Isn't it? We need never be in fear of an invader hearing our prayer of gentleness and sending a sword for an answer.

It's good to keep in mind, however, that according to the attitude of our prayer and not the words, we will attract attention. If our words are of kindness, but our attitude is of meanness, the providences that will hear will be ones of meanness, not kindness. It's the attitude of one who prays which determines the attraction, not the words.

What about meditation? *Meditation is really only silent prayer.* It's attentive, intense, silent prayer. As a form of prayer, it is highly worthwhile. Personally, I prefer informal meditation and not formal meditation, although I must admit that in the past, formal meditation has been an enjoyable and guiding experience. Formal meditation is only meditating with the aid of some prescribed verse. Informal meditation is merely meditating without such an aid – just letting your mind flow as it will, spontaneously and without prescribed course. I have enjoyed both types of meditation in my life, alone and with others, but the type I have used most is the informal type.

Collecting one's thoughts is always good; and for the most part, that is what meditation is. It's collecting your thoughts to better direct your life. It's examining what you are and who you are and where you are and why you are. It's pondering the four W's – What, Who, Where, and Why in order to find present position and direct future course.

When I was finding my way, the discipline of formal meditation via some written text was very useful, but now that I have found my way and myself and my direction, my prayer is almost completely informal – merely spontaneous. Now and then, I do recite out loud, but for the most part, I just ponder in silence. Reciting out loud, even if no one is around, however, can be terrific because it aids in the concentration of one's thinking. I have done a lot of recitation out loud when only hidden muses could hear. I have heard; and it has helped greatly in my forming my opinions and directing my life. Talking out loud, even if no one is there, can be a wonderful way to spend time because it adds to the focus of the moment.

When I was looking for my way, I'd emphasize petition as part of my prayer. In other words, I'd make it a routine to ask a favor of some real or imagined spiritual audience. Now, I recognize my providence and I are one and there's no need to ask for what my providence already knows I need. I do ask for favors in my prayers a little, but not a lot like I used to do. My needs are theirs; and theirs are mine. We're in this thing of life together and we have trust in one another. When trust is assumed, for the most part, petition prayer is unnecessary. On occasion, however, petition prayer is useful in terms of admitting to yourself by your prayer that others are about who can help. That's good to know, I'd say. Wouldn't you?

I used to be rather wordy in my prayers, but now I often have one little rather unique expression that tells my soul all of which I want to be reminded. It's a rather unintelligible expression, really, that says thank you to all my life's benefactors – from God to a man made faucet delivering water to me. Often people think I am grunting when I say it, but I am really full of gratitude for that which is about me at the moment and I say, *Huh, Huh!* as in *"Hmmmmmmmm – That's Good!"*

That little grunt sounding expression is often my total prayer – which is to illustrate that a prayer can be comprised of only one or two words or one or two sighs or a thousand words or whatever – or even an illiterate grunt. *Huh, Huh* says it for me quite often – and no one is aware that I just prayed. That little grunt, however, as an expression of a grateful heart, is a prayer at its finest. It's not how long one prays that is important. *It is the intention with which one prays that makes all the difference in the world.*

9

Secrets of the Soul

Where does the kingdom of souls exist? Wouldn't we all like to know the answer to that one? Is there another soul where you are right now, lurking about? Is there a friend in your midst you can't see, or an enemy? If so, where does he or she or it go when the visit ends? Can you be visited in a dream by another soul? Can another soul communicate with you in a dream state? I guess these are secrets of the soul; and we may never know the answers.

How do souls select bodies to take for their own? What controls the process? Are there more souls than bodies available? Or perhaps more bodies than souls? In abnormal situations, it seems that multiple souls can share the same body, but in normal situations or circumstances, it seems only one soul controls a body. Why is that? Is it that normally there is only room for one soul? If so, why is it there is room for more than one soul in abnormal situations? Or is that only an illusion? Is there only one soul in control at any given moment?

What should happen if my soul should leave my body for an astral adventure trip? Is it possible that while I am away, another soul could take possession and I'd be left homeless? And if another did take my body when I was away, would he take over the memory I left behind in my brain? I may be a coward, but I don't think I'll take the chance of trying to leave my body; leastwise not until I'm finished with it.

Where does the soul reside upon taking up residence in the body? Does it reside in the head, or the heart, or the genitals, or the shoulder, or all over? Does the soul grow with the growth of the body? That would not seem realistic if it enters the body as an existing entity, presumably as a mature soul upon incarnation – or reincarnation. Is the soul, then, elastic? Is it like one of those stockings where one size fits all?

How does an incarnated soul glean its information from a body? Do the senses communicate to it; and if so, how does it store the communication in its memory? Or does it even have a memory? It would seem likely that it does in order to link experiences from one life to another. How does the soul manage the images it receives? I suspect there are secrets of the soul for which we will never know the answers.

When a soul is free of the body, does it fly around? Does it feel anything? How does it move? What is its fuel? Where does it go? Does it get tired? Does it need to rest? Can it plan a day's activities with a community of souls? Do souls have parties? Do they join gangs?

Can they touch each other; or do they have to incarnate to do that?

How is a soul born of another soul, assuming it happens? It seems outrageous that a soul can give birth to another soul; but it seems more outrageous that it can't. Otherwise, how did my soul get started? We have already reviewed the alternatives; and none of them make much sense. There's no need to question the fact of a start; for I am living and got a start somehow. I don't question the start, just the how of the start; but I guess that, too, is a secret of the soul for which I'll never know the answer.

Did my soul come from a union or marriage of two other souls? Are souls sexy? That, too, seems preposterous; but then I guess all secrets are, leastwise all secrets of the soul.

And what about this thing called *destiny?* As I am writing (or "rewriting") this chapter, it is June 20, 2003. On the evening of June 17th, three days ago, just less than half a mile from where I sit, Walter and Betty and two grandsons, Scott and Bryan were on their way home to Oregon via I-80 West that goes by a community outside of Laramie, Wyoming called "Country Meadows" where I live. It was 5 in the evening. Moments before, there had been an accident which had stopped the traffic. Walter and Betty and Scott and Bryan were sitting in a pickup with a camper on the back of it and were the tail end of the stopped traffic. They were stopped behind a semi truck.

And then along came Ivan. He was in another semi truck traveling in the same lane as the lane in which

Walter and Betty and Scott and Bryan were stopped. Along side of Ivan was another semi truck. It all happened so quickly. When Ivan saw the stopped traffic ahead, his first notion was to change lanes, but the left lane was already occupied by a truck as large as his. And so Ivan took the path of least resistance, having no time to maneuver otherwise, and plowed into the pickup containing Walter and Betty and Scott and Bryan. They had no chance. Almost nothing was left of their pickup and camper after the collision; and Walter and Betty and Scott and Bryan had met their moment of final climax.

Was it their destiny to be the victims of a tragic accident on their way home to Oregon? Perhaps – and perhaps not. Perhaps it had been all "arranged" by the providence or providences of Walter and Betty and Scott and Bryan. Perhaps the accident up ahead had been also pre-arranged by the providences of these four. Perhaps it was a matter of providential timing rather than simply a matter of accidental happening. Who knows?

Souls come into this world and leave this world. Each of us needs an entry and each of us needs an exit. It could have been an accident that took the lives of Walter and Betty and Scott and Bryan – and then again, it could have been a conclusion to a kind of providential conspiracy. It wasn't God who took the lives of these four at this time because God is in us and not outside of us to make things happen like that; but it could have been a providence, a natural providence, not a divine providence, that arranged for Walter and

Betty and Scott and Bryan to be reunited with the community of souls from which they came. Maybe they all belonged to the same community; and maybe each of them belonged and belongs to a different community. Who knows?

But perhaps our destinies are among the many secrets of the soul – or secrets of souls. My father was killed on July 7th, 1966, standing on the side of a road. From my early teens, Dad told me periodically that he did not expect to live to see 60. When he passed, he was 59 and a half. A pickup came toward him traveling on the opposite side of the road. The driver fell asleep at the wheel, crossed over the road, and smashed into my father who should have been safe, standing on the opposite side of the road as he was. But maybe it was Dad's time – all arranged ahead of time. Maybe Dad's providence had decided it was time to "take him out"; and so they arranged for all the particulars of that day. Maybe it wasn't an accident; but an arrangement, a providential arrangement. Know what I mean? Who knows?

There's so much we don't know – and perhaps will never know. For some reason, fellow angel souls in the bodiless realm can't tell us the answers about them and us; or perhaps they just do not choose to do so.

I tell my soul and my soul tells me – don't be afraid. Life is not so fragile as we might think. No one can take a soul and control it, unless the owner let them. Your soul is your own and mine is mine; and neither of us should yield. We should share, yes, but not surrender.

Bodies may come and go and they are wonderful as miracles unto themselves, but souls probably go on and on. Thanks to the union of spirit and flesh, bodies can share with souls and souls with bodies; and the two together are perfect as each separately is perfect.

There are as many secrets of the soul, I think, as there are stars in the sky; but like the stars in the sky don't keep us from moving on and living and loving, neither should the secrets of the soul. Let the stars shine on; and let the secrets of the soul do the same.

Unmasking The Soul!

The End

I'm A Free Soul

By
Francis William Bessler
Laramie, Wyoming
8/8/2009

REFRAIN:
I'm a free soul. It's easy to be.
All I need to do – is know I belong to everything.
I'm a free soul - wandering where I will,
knowing all life is right
and in that knowledge, being fulfilled.

They ask me why in this world
I seem to get along
with everyone – and seem to be always
singing a happy song.
Refrain.

I ask why do others
not get along in this life.
I think it's because others
do not see all life as right.
Refrain.

How can anyone be truly free
who sees life as a pain –
and believes no one is good
and all should be constrained?
Refrain.

Love is not something, my Friend
that can be restricted to a few.
It's something you offer everyone
because everyone's the same as you.
Refrain.

Jesus lived a long time ago
and taught that Heaven is at hand.
That's because Heaven's only knowing
that God is where I stand.
Refrain.

All I need is to look about me
and the evidence is all around.
Wherever there's children playing,
it's where my heart is found.
Refrain.

The key to being free, I think,
is to know that you belong.
With that in mind, let me repeat
the message of this song.
Refrain (several times).

I'm A Happy Soul

By
Francis William Bessler
Laramie, Wyoming
12/18/2008

REFRAIN:
I'm a happy soul –
it's easy to be.
I just keep a smile on my face –
embracing the one that is me.
I'm a happy soul –
I try to greet everyone I meet,
thinking that each of us is Divine
and each of us must be complete.

Of course, it's to each his own,
but what makes me a happy one
is to know that somehow, I am Divine
and wonderfully a Divine son.
What keeps me happy is to realize
that you must share my Divinity.
More than anything else,
those are the notions that keep me free.
Refrain.

When I look out into the sky,
I can't imagine there can be an end;
and somehow that leads me to believe
that all of us should be friends.
How can there be more of what's endless
in the farthest galaxy?
But if it's all the same, then that tells me,
that the same should be free.
Refrain.

People live their entire lives
wondering where is God;
but if there is no end,
everywhere should find God in applause.
How can God be more where I am
than where you are, my friend?
So relax, and be aware,
Heaven must be where you stand.
Refrain (several times).

CHILD OF HUMANITY SERIES

By
Francis William Bessler
Laramie, Wyoming
- 2005 -

Introduction

This series is based on a title I came to know in 2004 – and absolutely love. In my favorite new book of 2004, *THE GOSPEL OF MARY (MAGDALENE)*, I was introduced to the concept of *"child of humanity."* Thus, I have named my series of 2005 after that notion. In brief, Jesus offers that I should look to the *"child of humanity"* within me to find the *"good news of the Kingdom."* I will explore that concept in essay # 5 of this series; however, in general, this series merely discusses the topics listed below as I see them. Along with *THE GOSPEL OF MARY*, I will also make significant reference to *THE GOSPEL OF THOMAS* as I explore the various topics included within my series.

About *THE GOSPEL OF THOMAS*, it was lost for over sixteen centuries, after being banned by the governmental and hierarchical institutions of the 4th Century. Prior to its being banned, it was one of many gospels that various people of the day referenced to gain an impression and understanding of Jesus; though, of course, there could not have been many copies of anything in those days for the lack of printing materials.

Let us just say that some ancient texts did exist and were the source of impressions about Jesus.

To the dismay of some, there was some conflict among the existing gospels. After Constantine came to power early in the 4th Century and became the Emperor of the Western World, he declared Christianity a state religion, but did not like the conflict among his bishops about the various impressions of Jesus. So, he bid his bishops to decide on those gospels that suited the power ones among them – since he was all about power himself – and then declared that all other gospels be banned – and even burned perhaps.

In the ensuing drama, the Gospels of Matthew, Mark, Luke, and John were selected to be the reigning gospels and all conflicting gospels like that of Thomas and Mary were charted to the dump heap. Though the various dumped gospels enjoyed their own individual dramas, and I suppose some were trashed as directed, some monk or other stashed *THE GOSPEL OF THOMAS* and some other banned material in a big jar and hid the jar in a cave off the Nile River in Egypt near what is known as Nag Hammadi. There that jar remained, unknown for centuries until a peasant in Egypt stumbled on the jar in 1945. That peasant had no idea of the contents of that jar, but it turned out to be some long lost and long hidden ancient manuscripts – among which was *THE GOSPEL OF THOMAS.* Theoretically, this Thomas is considered by many experts to be none other than Thomas, one of the twelve apostles of Jesus.

Though it is only speculation on my part, I suspect that Thomas may have written his work as notes he took down from Jesus during the life of Jesus. Since his work is nothing more than a bunch of *Jesus said* statements, it lends itself to being the possible note book of a student taking notes. Perhaps later, the others – Matthew through John – copied somewhat from those notes and then expanded them into a narrative. That is only a thought, however.

The ancient text of the work by Thomas, greatly deteriorated over the years, was written in Coptic, an Egyptian language. The original work was likely written in Greek since it has been speculated that Thomas was Greek. Perhaps Thomas was a student from Greece, just chancing upon Jesus – or perhaps Thomas knew Jesus from an earlier age – perhaps before the so called public ministry of Jesus. Before that public ministry from about the age of thirty, nothing is offered about Jesus in the regular gospels, except a few boyhood references. Perhaps Thomas knew Jesus before Peter and the others knew him, though the regular gospels offer Jesus meeting Thomas after the start of his public ministry. It is hard to say.

Since the finding in 1945, there have been numerous translations I suppose; but my first look at **THE GOSPEL OF THOMAS** came in 1979 from a book copyrighted in 1959. To my knowledge, the source I have used is likely the first translation. It was translated by a team of scholars headed by a fellow named A. Guillaumont. I like to think Mr. Guillaumont's translation is the most authentic, being the first and being without subsequent corruption of original text.

Like any process of translation and interpretation, verses tend to change ever so slightly with each process. As an example, in Verse 37 (of 114) of Mr. Guillaumont's translation, Jesus is asked by his disciples when he will be known. To that question, Mr. Guillaumont's edition has Jesus answering *when you take off your clothing without being ashamed.* I do not have the name of the translator handy at the moment, but one translation I read had Jesus answering that question with **"when you strip yourself of shame."** I may be wrong, but I suspect Mr. Guillaumont's translation tried to translate the Coptic words as found, but the other translation chose instead to interpret the translation – not actually translate the words.

And, of course, that is a major problem with various translations of any foreign text. We may not get a translation of the text itself, but an assumed interpretation of a translation. Why would the second source offer that we would recognize Jesus when we strip ourselves of shame and not offer the original text of *when you take off your clothing without being ashamed?* Probably because he did not want to get into a discussion about nakedness. He assumed that Jesus was only offering that we have to be without shame to recognize him and that really has nothing to do with nakedness, per se; however for one, I disagree completely. I think Jesus meant exactly what Mr. Guillaumont had him say. All Jesus is saying is that shame is not recognizing the divinity of nakedness. That is, in my opinion, that is so. How can you talk about the divinity of nakedness or the shamelessness of nakedness without referring to nakedness itself?

Well, many think you can – and so they do. Perhaps it offers a good lesson about accepting what we find in any translation. How in the world can we know a translation is literal unless we are familiar with the source foreign language? I cannot. I must admit that. I have no knowledge whatever of Coptic. For all I know, the second source may have had it right and the first source, Mr. Guillaumont, may have been the guilty one of offering nakedness as an expression of shamelessness. Still, the greater likelihood is that the earliest translation is probably the most literal because initial scholars are far more interested in translating words rather than ideas. Until I know different, I will always retain the 1959 translation as the first and most authentic of all translations of *THE GOSPEL OF THOMAS.*

Concerning my other favorite long lost gospel, *THE GOSPEL OF MARY,* according to my source on that one, Marvin Meyer - who included *THE GOSPEL OF MARY* within a general work that deals with all the gospels that may have had some bearing on Mary Magdalene – *THE GOSPEL OF MARY* was probably banned and hidden like *THE GOSPEL OF THOMAS;* however the site of hiding was not Nag Hammadi. I have no idea where it was hidden, but as early as the late 19th Century, it was found in something called the Berlin Gnostic Codex. Mr. Meyer does not offer it was found in the late 19th Century in his work called

THE GOSPELS OF MARY, but it is my understanding from some other source I read that such is so. Like *THE GOSPEL OF THOMAS, THE GOSPEL OF MARY* was also found in Coptic. The original author of *THE GOSPEL OF MARY* is suspected to be Mary Magdalene – and it may have been written in the late 1st Century or early 2nd Century, quite likely again in Greek.

Mr. Meyer's work was copyrighted in 2004. So, it is very new – unlike the 1959 copyright of *THE GOSPEL OF THOMAS* or *THE GOSPEL ACCORDING TO THOMAS*, authored by Mr. A. Guillaumont and team. Mr. Meyer offers in his work that some earlier texts of *THE GOSPEL OF MARY* may have been in Greek – and there seems to be some fragments in Greek somewhere – but the most complete version was in Coptic. Even so, that Coptic version is missing several pages at the front and also several pages in the middle – perhaps due to corruption of aging.

The dating and actual authorship of any gospel, however, is largely a matter of speculation. Who is to say for sure who wrote what and when any of it was actually written? As earlier noted, some scholars speculate that the gospels of Thomas and Mary Magdalene were written in the late 1st Century or early 2nd Century; but, if so, it would be almost impossible that the actual authors could have been the Apostle, Thomas, or the Apostle, Mary Magdalene because they would have been much too old for such authorship. They would have had to have been near or over 100 years of age. How likely is that? It would be conceivable, however, that others could have written the gospels using the names of Thomas and Mary Magdalene while copying from some earlier jottings of Thomas and/or Mary. Who knows? But who knows when and by whom any of the gospels were written?

I have noticed, too, among several "interpretations" of *THE GOSPEL OF MARY,* a similar disparity between translations as I found in separate versions of *THE GOSPEL OF THOMAS.* In the translation (interpretation) offered by Mr. Meyer, Jesus offers that we should look for the *child of humanity* within us to find peace. In a different – and again unknown – source, the translation of interpretation has Jesus offering that we should look for the **"son of man"** within us to find peace – not Mr. Meyer's *child of humanity.* Why would one call it the **son of man** and the other call it *child of humanity?*

Who knows? But I identify with *child of humanity,* not **son of man,** because I see a very important lesson in the term. It is not that I could not get my lesson out of **"son of man,"** but I think it is clearer understood as *child of humanity.* Since Jesus often referred to himself in the regular gospels as **"son of man,"** it is better to go with the more generic term of *child of humanity* so as not to confuse it with Jesus.

Be that as it may, you now have a glimpse at the meaning of the discussions offered in this series of essays. Essentially, I will be looking for answers among the **Gospels of Thomas and Mary** as I pace through the topics I cover. The version of *THE GOSPEL OF MARY* I will use will be that offered by Marvin Meyer in his work *THE GOSPELS OF MARY.* I hope he does not mind. If I thought it is an infringement on his copyright of the translation I use, I would not use the text in his book without his permission, but as I see it, any ancient gospel ought to be public domain. The same goes for my use of Mr. A. Guillaumont's work of *THE GOSPEL ACCORDING TO THOMAS.* Those texts do not belong to just some, but to all because they were probably written for all – though because of the accident of certain history, they were kept away from the public for centuries.

With that in mind, the various subjects explored in the series are:

I will feature the various essays almost exactly like I featured them in separate essays that I shared with some as I wrote them – from January to August of 2005.

For this work, I have added this ***INTRODUCTION*** to introduce ***THE GOSPELS OF THOMAS*** and ***MARY***; but from here on, the essays are as I wrote them originally.

Thanks! FWB
August, 2005

1

Returning to a Circular Christianity

1/2/2005

Imagine, if you will, a round table with four legs holding up the middle and making a bit of a square in the center of the round table. Now, imagine that some carpenter arrives at the scene and decides to make the round table a square table and cuts off everything exceeding the square in the middle of the table, including an extra four legs stationed underneath the borders of the round table top. Instead of seating twelve people around the table, the new table only seats four.

Now, imagine that the table top represents Jesus; and the legs represent the various visions or interpretations of Jesus. With the carpenter making a much smaller square where previously a larger circle existed, the table of Jesus takes on a completely different look and a completely narrowed vision. Only the visions of

Jesus represented by the square in the middle remain; and with the restriction of visions or interpretations of Jesus to just four, Jesus himself takes on a new look in general.

In my opinion, this is what happened to the table of Jesus and Christianity in the 4th Century when only four books offering an interpretation were selected. By restricting any vision of Jesus to just the four seemingly in the middle of the former circle of Jesus, we – the world – lost a lot of table space and a whole lot of the full picture of Jesus. Those in the middle, of course, hold that the extended visions or versions of Jesus were not acceptable to them; and, thus, they do not miss them; but what about all of those who represented what might be called an "extended" vision of Jesus? They were dismissed to the cold and told they did not matter. Most importantly, however, by cutting off the legs of some of the former circular table, Jesus himself became like a body amputated of some of his limbs. The result is we have suffered a kind of corruption of Jesus in terms of some of the visions and interpretations that once existed were suspended.

In a rather figurative fashion, I think this is what happened in the 4th Century. Previous to Emperor Constantine deciding to make Christianity a state religion, it was a circle with lots of different visions of Jesus allowed to sit around the table. When Emperor Constantine decided to reduce the table in order to make it more manageable from a ruler's standpoint, at least half of the total makeup of a former Christianity was lost. Under the guidance and directive of Constantine, various interpretations of Jesus were out-lawed. Matthew, Mark, Luke, and John – the alleged four pillars in the middle – were retained; and many legs like those of Thomas, Mary Magdalene, Philip, and various others were lopped off.

Currently, I belong to the Unitarian Church. In this church, we are permitted to have many different views of life. I suspect it could be said that none of us holds the exact same opinions about life as the next person, sitting around what is a circular table; but our differences are not only allowed, but encouraged. The *Unitarian Experience*, if it could be called that, is proof to me that we can all get together and get along and not have to hold the same views.

My particular love is of Jesus, but others don't find him all that appealing. Perhaps some of my fellow Unitarians might wish that I would sit down and shut up about Jesus. Well, I may sit down, but I will not shut up. And if I did shut up, the very wholesome greater experience of Unitarianism would not be fulfilled. My fellow Unitarians need for me to still speak up for my vision of Jesus to offer a part of the general picture of various visions of life; and I need for them to speak up for their views as well. In the end, it all works fabulously well.

Restricting the discussion to Jesus alone, however, by the acts and decisions of King Constantine and his selected bishops who decided that the canon of the *BIBLE* should be restricted to the four of Matthew,

Mark, Luke, and John - for many centuries, Jesus has been lost. He has been lost because a fuller vision of him with all the various possible complexities about him has been outlawed.

When I was growing up, I had no idea that more than four versions of Jesus had ever existed. I belonged quite cuddly to that four square thing in the middle of a former circular table. Not knowing there were any additional versions, I was wonderfully happy dealing with the Jesus who was taught to me by my church – Catholicism. Later in life, I discovered a great truth. Originally, the table of Jesus had been much larger than anything I could have imagined. That table of Jesus was so large as to even allow the unthinkable to a four square gospel person such as me. Some who had known Jesus actually found him not to be the redeemer I had been told he had to be. Some who had known Jesus actually challenged the concept of what is called in traditional Christianity, original sin – the very center of the Christianity that was allowed to survive.

Many might say – that's preposterous! Surely, you can't possibly claim that something as fundamental to Christian thought as original sin might not be true. How could a Christian possibly believe in the lack of original sin? Did not Jesus come to expose and dispose of original sin? Well, that is one version of him, yes, that belonging to the four square proposition in the middle of a former circular table. But, yes, it is actually true that some who believed themselves to be as Christian as the four square people in the middle actually took issue with original sin – the very heart beat of traditional Christianity. At least, such is implied, if not expressed, to me in one of the gospels, commended to the trash heap by Constantine and his disciples.

In the forbidden *GOSPEL OF MARY*, Jesus is asked about sin. To clarify Mary, it is widely believed that this Mary is none other than Mary Magdalene. My, My! If the author of *THE GOSPEL OF MARY* is really Mary Magdalene, one of those declared by Constantine and his disciples to be a heretic is none other than perhaps one of Jesus's best friends, Mary Magdalene. Anyway, in *THE GOSPEL OF MARY*, Jesus is asked about sin. His response: *There is no such thing as sin, except that you create it, as in adultery*. You may think of that as a rather flippant and irrelevant claim, but imagine the consequences if it is actually true.

What now happens to the favored idea of Jesus being some kind of needed redeemer to save us from a terrible sin that, in fact, we do not have? That rather upends the whole notion of Jesus. Doesn't it? If I am to believe that a gospel of Mary actually existed, however, that is entirely a possibility. If it is true, would you not agree that such a thought could have an unbelievable impact on Christianity? Think of all the souls – like myself now – who could actually go with that program rather than the issued program of original sin we have all inherited.

If Mary really got Jesus right, though others are free to interpret her gospel differently, Jesus probably believed that inherited sin is nonsense. He probably believed that sin exists alright, but as products of our own creation, having no essential dependence on being inherited. If Mary is right, for instance, Paul is wrong. Paul says that we are all born in sin and inherit it and only Jesus can expel it from us. Then Mary, sitting at the edge of the table, says, in paraphrase: *I disagree.* **My master never believed we are all born of sin and are in an inherited state of sin. He believed that sin is not an inheritance, but rather a creation of ourselves.**

Down through history, however, the various churches of Christianity have dictated that no one has a right to not believe in original sin. It has been considered the very center of Christianity and Christian thought. Until I discovered that other gospels about Jesus existed that were banned and damned by 4th Century rulers, I had no idea that it could be possible. Now, the cat is out of the bag. Call it a product of our "information age." Now we know the truth. Originally, before the amputation process of Constantine and his disciples, Christianity contained vastly more interpretations of life than was allowed to pass into the 5th Century.

Somehow, not all the versions of Jesus that were banned were actually destroyed. In 1945, some ignorant peasant stumbled, completely by accident, on some jars hidden in a cave off the Nile River in Egypt. These jars contained many ancient manuscripts written in Coptic, an Egyptian language – including the gospels of Thomas and Philip. That is supposedly Thomas, the Apostle of Jesus. And with the new unearthing of Thomas and many other interpretations of Jesus, the once circular table of Christianity can now go back to its size, prior to Constantine and his disciples.

Anyway, that is my vision of the future. I see it happening – not because I am writing about it, but because I am somewhat part of the huge process that is now taking place. Like the **Unitarian Experience** proves, we do not have to believe in the same doctrines to get along. We can return to the yesteryear of Christianity and begin to take back what Constantine and his disciples took away. We can expand Christianity from its long allowed four square restricted table to its former circular table; and with that allowance, we can start to sit twelve around a table where heretofore, only four have been allowed to sit. The **Unitarian Experience** proves it can work; and as I write here today, I hope – and think - it is happening.

Where will we go with a restored *Circular Christianity?* Eventually, everywhere perhaps. I do not know. All that I know now is that with the loss of what might be termed the gospels of an extended Christianity, we have probably been missing Jesus for a long, long time. In the debate over who the real Jesus was, it was arbitrarily decided that Jesus should be defined as necessary redeemer, the fulfillment of a promised Jewish Messiah. It was one of the views of Jesus, but it was not the only one. I think it would be extremely useful to restore the full discussion - welcoming Thomas and Mary and Philip and others around the table - and let those of the current age decide the issue once again.

2

Sin

2/4/2005

I am not one to beat about the bush. I am convinced that humanity, but especially Christianity, has been way off the beaten path in terms of ideal virtue – or practicing it. That which I would call a betrayal of Christianity, or if you will, Christ – and true virtue - began and still continues with a misunderstanding of sin.

Correct me if I am wrong. According to traditional Christianity, sin can be defined as a transgression against God. Am I right or wrong? Surely we can agree that if sin is not really a transgression against God, almost all Christian religion has been based from almost the beginning on a false premise. I maintain that is exactly the case. I maintain that the very definition of sin as traditionally understood is wrong – and not only wrong, but tragically so. If we cannot even get the real definition of sin right, what in the world are we doing pretending to get virtue right?

Can sin possibly be a transgression against God? I would say it is possible only if God can be violated. Would you not agree? If God cannot be violated, then neither can anyone sin against God. Right? So, it seems to me, an initial burden of a thinking person is to resolve for him or herself the matter of violation of God. What can be a violation of God? If I violate you, I take away something from you. Could it be different with God? If I violate God, then it must be that I take away something from Him or Her or It.

Assuming that you have such a power to take away something from God, tell me what it could be. You say I can violate God. That means I can steal something from "Him." Think about it. If God is everywhere, as most people claim God is, how could God lose anything? If you think of God as being a being that is another being – though a "Supreme Being" – then I suppose you could conjure the possibility of God being able to lose something. In practice, that is exactly what most folks who believe in the traditional concept of sin do. They define God as a Supreme Being, implying that God is a being over all other beings, but inside of none.

In my current view of the matter, however, any **Supreme Being** that is not also in everything is not a God, but only a god. Thus the Jewish/Christian God is not a God, but only a god – from which potential property can be stolen. In truth, however, God is not a god from whom a possession can be stolen. God is really an Infinite Presence from which nothing can be stolen. If God is not a supreme being god, merely better than all other beings, but is a God that is necessarily in everything, then sin as defined as a transgression against God is null and void.

What did Jesus have to say about the matter? It is hard to say if you are asking that question and expecting an answer from any of the canonical gospels. Matthew through John talk a lot about sin, but never define what it is. Look for yourself if you doubt me. Sin is merely portrayed as any conduct that might violate what may be called the Kingdom of God. That Kingdom is never defined as such either. It is no wonder that humans have lived for thousands of years hoping to belong to a Kingdom for which they have no real clear understanding. It has been like we have been on some kind of journey toward some unknown destination for which assumed maps have been provided by anyone who wants to claim that he or she knows the way to the Kingdom. Yet none of us have actually been to the assumed Kingdom in order to be sure of the way to it.

If an acceptable definition of the Kingdom of God cannot be found in Matthew through John of the **BIBLE,** is there some definition somewhere else in some other gospel that might provide a lead? I think so. In **THE GOSPEL ACCORDING TO THOMAS,** Jesus says in Verse 3: *The Kingdom is within you and without you. If you know yourselves, you will be known and you will know that you are sons of the Living Father.* The other gospels say this in some degree, too, but they also take great pains to point out that Jesus was a special son of the Living Father and even go so far as to say that Jesus was and is **the only son of the Living Father.**

Assuming that *The Living Father* of **THE GOSPEL OF THOMAS** is really referring to God, Thomas has Jesus telling his disciples that they (and we?) are all sons of the Living Father. He makes no claim whatsoever about being an only son. He does, however, emphasize our need to know that we are sons of the Living Father. If we know ourselves, we will know we are sons of the Living Father; but not knowing that we are sons of the Living Father does not make us outside the Kingdom. It only makes us ignorant of our true status; but it does not deflate our true status.

In Verse 3 of **THE GOSPEL OF THOMAS**, Jesus says the Kingdom is *within you and without you*. That is only to say *the Kingdom is everywhere*. If the Kingdom is everywhere, then there can be no place where the Kingdom is not. If that is so, being already in the Kingdom we seek elsewhere, we probably will never find it anywhere.

In another verse of **THE GOSPEL ACCORDING TO THOMAS,** verse 113, Jesus says: *the Kingdom of the Father is spread upon the earth and men do not see it.* Why? Because the Kingdom of the Father – the Kingdom of God – is everywhere. What does this nice little idea do to the idea that sin is a transgression against God? For me, it completely annihilates it. How can anyone transgress against God – or the Kingdom of God – if no one can ever be expelled from it? And how can anyone ever be expelled from the Kingdom of God if that Kingdom is everywhere?

I hope we have proceeded to decide that the traditional idea of sin cannot be correct. That is really an important step; but if sin is not a transgression against God, can it be something else?

Once again, we just happen to have another of the expelled gospels coming to our rescue. In **THE GOSPEL OF MARY** (Magdalene?), Jesus is asked about sin. In Verse 1 of that outlawed and forbidden gospel: *Peter said to him, "You have explained everything to us. Tell us also, what is the sin of the world?" The savior replied, "There is no such thing as sin, but you create sin when you mingle as in adultery, and this is called sin.*

It has been taught down through the ages of Christendom that sin is inherited all the way from Adam and Eve. In this verse, Jesus clearly repudiates that notion. As importantly, however, Jesus in **THE GOSPEL OF MARY** tries to clarify that sin has to do with finite relations only and at least implies it does not have anything to do with a relationship with the Infinite or God. We sin when we mingle, as in adultery; but our sin is only against a fellow creature, not God.

We have already determined that no one can sin against God because no one can steal anything from an omnipresent God. It seems to me that the Jesus of Mary is telling us what sin is, not what sin is not. We sin when we mingle improperly. That is what he is saying. Mingling, as in adultery, I think can be taken as **improper mingling**. Adultery is an example of improper mingling. But at least we now have a real definition of sin. No longer are we out there flailing against the wind trying to figure out how we have violated a God that cannot be violated. If nothing else, that is tremendous progress.

The hints of this lesson have been there all along in the gospels of Matthew through John of the **BIBLE**. Jesus constantly warns against that which I call **improper mingling** in that he constantly emphasizes the need for compassion. If you have true compassion for all beings – not just human - then you cannot violate another individual. Compassion – true compassion – the main dictation of the regular gospels – says what needs to be said; but in stripping all members of life of divinity, except Jesus, compassion has been much harder to come by.

If we want to call it a sin, perhaps the greatest sin of all has been conducted by those in life who have based their entire livelihoods on a lie that not all are divine. The reason this is such a great sin is that by leaving us without a sense of true esteem, we have been led to act just like the senseless, sinful, rebels the sin mongers have accused us of being. Their great sin is that we have lived up to the reputation they have defined us as having. Though they do not sin against God, anymore than any of us can, they sin against the world by leading the world to believe it is less than it is.

And what is the world? The world of Nature, that is. Every single item, every single son, every single daughter, every single thing is a *son of the Living Father*. To be unaware of such a great heritage and identity is to act in blindness, living in the middle of a Paradise that is never known. What is sin? It is believing and acting like one is sinful by nature. It is believing and acting like one needs salvation from divinity. It is believing and acting like there is inequality in divinity and that somehow God can choose some to be more divine than others. That is sin. It can be forgiven only by replacing it with virtue. No other forgiveness is needed or useful. True forgiveness of sin is only finally recognizing what it really is – and stopping it. Begging for pardon and imagining its deliverance is not forgiveness. That is only a continuation of sin.

What is virtue? The opposite of sin, of course. **It is believing and acting like one is holy by nature. It is believing and acting like one is dressed in divinity because all things are dressed in divinity, being all in God. It is believing and acting like there is equality in all beings because all beings are equal in God.** Let us always be mindful that sin is an act and a belief, not a condition.

Like Jesus says in the canonical gospels – *Now, go and sin no more!*

3

Heaven

3/1/2005

Without sin, there is ? What is the answer to that?
Of course, one has to define sin in order to be able
to answer the question. So, let us retreat to the previous article for a definition. Others may have their
own definitions of sin, but since I am the one talking
about it here, then it should be according to my
definition.

What is sin? It is believing and acting like one is sinful by nature. It is believing and acting like one needs
salvation from divinity. It is believing and acting like
there is inequality in divinity and that somehow God
can choose some to be more divine than others. That
is sin.

Well, that is how I put it then. In the previous article, I argued that there is no such thing as sin – as Jesus
would have put it – except that we create it in our minds
and give it life. Anyone with an imagination can do

that, you know. Anyone with an imagination can bring something to life and make it exist in mind – even if it does not actually exist in reality; but that which exists in the mind may as well exist in reality for the individual who thinks it because for him or her, it is reality.

When it comes to sin, it is something that cannot exist in reality in terms of there being an actual possibility of a separation between God and anything. God is Infinite; and, as such, must be everywhere. Since sin is traditionally understood as separation from God, if sin exists at all, it can only exist in a virtual mode. It can only exist in the minds that may think about it. It cannot exist in reality – insofar as it being defined as a separation from God.

Now, back to our original question: Without sin, there is ? How would you answer that question? I would answer it – Heaven. Without sin, there is Heaven. It naturally follows then that if there can be no place where there is sin – or an actual absence of God – there can be no place that is not Heaven; for Heaven is only being in the Presence of God.

As Jesus says in *THE GOSPEL OF THOMAS, The Kingdom of the Father is spread upon the earth and men do not see it.* The Kingdom of the Father in this instance is Heaven. What more can be said about it? It is what it is. Heaven must be right where I am sitting right now. Heaven must be right where you are sitting – or standing – right now. As Jesus might say, there are many different rooms and a variety of life in those many rooms, but all of those rooms, as various as they are, are Heaven because God is in them all.

People, I think, have a very mistaken notion about morality, in terms of thinking that Heaven is dependent upon it. Many, if not most, are convinced that morality is a God imposed thing. God imposes a rule that all must obey and immorality is, in essence, defying the rule of God.

First of all, there is no rule of God as such that any finite thing can define – other than the overriding rule that **God must be everywhere**. If there are rules that are advanced to mankind via any so called prophet, you can be sure that if they offer any kind of a threat that suggests that anyone can be exempted from God or that God can dismiss anyone, you can be sure it is only a god that is speaking through a prophet and not God. **A god is a being separate from another that acts to own or control that other.** *God is not a god because It is not separate from another, though by nature, all beings are under the control of God in that all things are just as they are created to be; but most importantly, God is not a god because It is not separate from another that may be within It's control.*

I am often criticized for sticking to the use of the word God for referencing the Infinite One. I don't know what other word to use. So I stick with God. I see **"God"** as an abbreviation of *"Good."* I do not know if the originator of the word God meant it that way; but practically speaking, that is how I see God – as That Good or Goodness from which all things come and in which all things reside. It is perhaps a bit unfortunate that some do not mean that definition when they refer to God; but it is my definition and I intend to stick with it.

Continuing with a little discussion of immorality, in effect, immorality is only doing that which is hurtful to myself. I am immoral when I act in a self-destructive manner. I may also act in a way that destroys another; but, per se, it is not my destroying another for what that does to the other that is immoral – related to my self. **Immorality should be very self centered because it is not what I do to another that matters most in the end, but what I do to myself; but – and here's the crux of it – what I do to you, I do to me.**

If, with premeditation, I kill you, it is an expression of my trying to kill something in me. I am only using you as a tool to get at me. I am dealing with myself by using you as a substitute for myself. Otherwise, I would not set out to kill, no matter what the motivation. If I am concentrated on some other intent – like to be kind at all costs – then there is no way I can want to kill you, no matter what you may have done. If people want to kill, in the end, it is because they lack motivation to be kind.

There are many gods, but only one God. Gods (gods) can pretend to be of God; and they often do in order to restrict behavior to a desired pattern; but people should not be fooled by gods claiming to represent God. Many gods make rules that may form some sort of morality – or impose some sort of morality; but if God is everywhere and in everything, there should never be a question of pleasing or displeasing the only

God as an expression of a morality. In a sense, God is immoral in terms of anything that might be expected of any created being. **Creation itself is a Divine Thing, but Creation is not caught up with the individual behaviors of created things.**

Just look at general creation if you do not know of that which I speak. God creates a lion and God creates a deer. The lion eats the deer; but that does not make the lion immoral related to God. It only makes the lion immoral related to the deer. Between the lion and the deer there may be some sort of morality in terms of one dealing with the other; but since God made – and makes – both the lion and the deer, related to God, there is no immorality when the lion eats the deer.

Likewise, you may kill me; and for me, that is an immorality in that something is happening to me that I do not like; but it may also be an immorality for you because you may be doing far more harm to yourself than to me by killing me. If you kill once, you may kill again because by killing once, you are establishing a pattern. **The real judgment of any morality is that patterns established must be continued.** If you kill me and do it for no reason other than anger, chances are you will not see behind your anger and you will kill again – and again – and again – and again. Keep in mind, too, that anger in itself is a form of murder. So by being angry now, you will likely retain your anger the next moment – and the next moment – and the next moment – and the next moment; but the one you are murdering most is yourself because it is you that you have to abide.

Keep in mind, too, as Jesus pointed out, our virtual reality is much more a thing of thought than deed. Accordingly, if I hate you, but do not kill you, I am still guilty in a way of killing you because that is the trend of my thoughts. It does not matter if I kill you or not. If I want to kill you, the law of virtual reality says that I am guilty of doing what I think about. It is my disposition that is my judge; and my disposition is mostly a matter of mind. **It matters little if I actually do what I am disposed to do. It only matters that I am disposed to do it.**

Not to be sidetracked, however, Heaven has nothing to do with any of that. *Heaven is merely the Presence of God.* You can be in Heaven and not know it; and most folks go through their lives, I think, failing to realize that they are in Heaven. They think of Heaven in terms of reward for some morality. Well, people have a right to define Heaven as they like, but for me, it is not reward for morality, but **merely a Presence of God.** Moral or immoral, related to any supposed regimen, I am in Heaven.

Now, if you want to talk about sin related to some artificial morality, imposed by some god or other, be it Christian, Jewish, Islamic, or whatever and offer that Heaven is the reward for obeying a morality, then you have a different Heaven than I. That which you call Heaven, I may simply call **Home** in terms of where my soul wants to reside and with whom it wants to reside. But my **home** may not be your home and your home may not be mine – even as both your home and mine are in Heaven.

Heaven is where God is. That is my definition of it. It is not where some god is. Heaven has nothing to do with such a one. It is simply where God is. Since God is everywhere, then Heaven is everywhere. Home, in terms of any given disposition, is where you are and where those who love you are. By your disposition, you choose your home, but by your disposition, you do not choose Heaven.

That merely indicates how important it is to choose the right home for you. Your soul, like my soul, is attracted to like souls. If I want to be an angry soul, all I have to do is be angry; and presto, I will be surrounded by angry souls. Then anger becomes my home and the home of all my companion souls. Most people, I think, have a bad sense of judgment in that they think it will be delved out by God or a god; but the truth of it is, we delve ourselves our own judgment by choosing a disposition; and, as it is often put, *we reap what we sow.* If we go forward with a kind disposition, then kindness will be our disposition. If we go forward with an angry disposition, then anger will be our disposition. It is really straight forward.

I think it is good to keep all this in mind as we pass through life. Life itself is filled with mystery; and because it is, many gods like to pretend to be God in offering some explanation of a mystery with but one objective in mind – to gain control of another soul. Since children of God, in general, are not aware of the details of any mystery, any god who wants to impose some arbitrary rule or other and claim it comes from God can often get away with it.

Show me your credentials! That is what we should demand of anyone claiming to be of God. How do I know you are from God and not just from some god pretending to be God? If they answer, I am from God because I am in the spirit of God, well what can I say? **Everyone is in the spirit of God; and being in the spirit of God – or the presence of God – is no excuse for claiming divine rule.**

Most importantly, however, for this issue of my *CHILD OF HUMANITY SERIES*, Heaven is only **being in the presence of God.** Knowing that, if we are smart, we will begin this very moment to stop waiting for Heaven to happen. It is already happening because God is already here. There is no need to wait. Look at yourself and see the miracle you are. You are no different than me in terms of being an individual miracle of God. We are different in our individuality, but in God we are the same. God is the Father or Mother or Parent of us both. Assume that – and life can be made easy because **if you fill your heart with gratitude for what you are, you can have no room for dissatisfaction and unhappiness.**

Heaven is where you are – and where you will be. Why not enjoy it?

4

Brother Jesus

4/4/2005

Preface

The rules have changed. We have progressed since Jesus walked this earth 2,000 years ago. It is not that Jesus has changed. It is that we have changed. In the 2,000 years since Jesus walked this earth, God has evolved. That is, our notions of God have evolved – at least for many of us. When Jesus walked this earth, we had the idea that man and God were separated. With that idea, we felt we needed some kind of bonding agent to stick us together – or back together. Naturally, having a sense of separation from God, we needed a messiah. We needed someone who could heal the division. We needed someone who could resolve the impasse. We needed someone who could make us one with God. So, it was only natural with our thinking that we were separated from God that we needed a Jesus to be our messiah – to save us from the Godless dungeon of a divine less jungle.

Well, things have changed. We no longer think we are in a divine less jungle – at least many of us do not. Now we realize that if God is really Infinite, then God must be truly everywhere. What does that do to the separation idea upon which we formulated our need for a messiah ruling? Of course, it tosses it out the window. It throws it under the trampling hoofs of a runaway herd of bawling cattle – racing not to the edge of a cliff – but out to a brand new pasture. This is the world we have today. No longer do we feel God is "out there." Many of us at least have God in our hearts and in our chests and in our minds and in our gardens and in our wives and in our husbands and in our children and in every single thing. So if we are no longer separated from God – or have progressed to the realization that whatever God is, God is not gone from us - no longer do we need a messiah. The truth, of course, is that we never did need a messiah because there never was a breach between God and man; but be that as it may, mindfully at least, we live in a different world now than the world in which Jesus walked.

That means we have to find a different realization for Jesus – if we want to keep him at all. I want to keep him because I have long believed he was falsely miscast as a messiah in the first place. I want to keep him because I get the sense in *THE GOSPEL OF THOMAS* that he begged his fellow Jews to not cast him in the role of savior – the role of messiah; but the Mel Gibson directors of the day wanted him as their main star and they would have nothing else. So when Jesus died, they ignored his pleas to not make him a messiah and called on the ghost of Jesus to star as The Messiah – even though the real, throbbing, living Jesus begged to be excluded from that role when he was alive.

In **THE GOSPEL OF THOMAS** (Verse 52), one of those who wanted to cast Jesus as messiah said to Jesus: *Twenty-four prophets spoke in Israel and they all spoke about (lit:in) Thee.* That was their way of telling him that he was chosen to play the lead in their Messiah Play. Did Jesus answer that he wanted the role? Judge for yourself. *He said to them: You have dismissed the Living (One) who is before you and you have spoken about the dead.* The Living One, of course, is Jesus. Jesus did not want to be linked to the "dead" because by doing so, he was being dismissed for the true independent teacher he really was. Who could have been the "dead" that Jesus was referencing? That has to be "the twenty four prophets." Right? The twenty four prophets had no idea that God and man are one. They lived with the idea that God is outside of us and that they needed to sacrifice dead animals to their god in order to keep their god somewhat in their presence – to keep him from straying too far a field.

But Jesus begged us not to cast him in the lot of the twenty four prophets who thought they needed a messiah. He knew that God is not outside of us and he knew there is no need for a messiah; but those who bowed down to the twenty four prophets and their demand for a messiah had no such perspective. They needed a messiah – and damn it – Jesus could not refuse the role. He had to play it. So **when Jesus died, his ghost was given the role that the living Jesus denied in life.**

Such is the prelude to this week's issue of my Child of Humanity Series. We have evolved now from the time of Jesus. We have grown to realize that the living Jesus was right – the twenty four prophets of Israel are dead and they should remain dead. We are not to listen to them anymore. We have a new realization of God – and with our new realization of God – we have a brand new Jesus. With that, with the need of a brand new Jesus, let us carry on the discussion about who Jesus really is. The God and man separation issue has drained down the sink now like a litter of ten day old stinking garbage. With the stench gone forever from our lives, let us proceed.

Looking for a New Jesus

Was Jesus a king? For the many familiar with the alleged life of Jesus, there was a title placed over his head on the cross on which he died. That plaque read: *JESUS – KING OF THE JEWS.*

How little we know of Jesus to think that he was a king – or could ever be a king. Kings control. Kings rule. Jesus could not control; and Jesus can never rule. If, in fact, Jesus was crucified, he was crucified because he could not rule. He was crucified because he could not power himself over another to prevent it. If he died as they say he did in the gospels, he died without resistance to save himself and to show us the true nature of salvation – which is only another word for **freedom**. He did not die to become a king – not then or ever.

Let me offer you a little exercise. I want you to take your left hand, curl those fingers toward you. Now take your right hand and curl those fingers toward you. Then put both hands in front of you with arms extended outward and let the curled fingers of both hands clasp each other. Now, without relaxing, pull one hand from the other. If you are doing as I am asking, given that the strength of your left and right hands are equal, you will not be able to pull them apart. What does that say? Is your left hand free? Is your right hand free? No! Of course not! And that is what happens when one soul controls another. Neither the controller nor the controlled one is free.

If I hold you to me, I am not free – and neither are you. To be in control or to be a ruler of another is to be without freedom. There has never been a king who has ever been free because kings control; but in controlling, they are controlled by the ones they control. This is the amazing truth of freedom. No one can be free who is either controlled by another or controls another. Like a left hand pulling against a right hand, neither hand is free.

Now, tell me, do you think Jesus would give up his freedom to control you, to rule you? Little do you know Jesus if you think that Jesus would give up his freedom to become your king. It is terribly sad to say that in the days of Jesus almost no one knew him for the champion of freedom he was. Jesus came to challenge those who think they have a right to impose a rule over another – like the Jews of his day. The Jews were embossed in law – and bossed by it. Many who have no inkling of who Jesus really was think that Jesus came to perfect the law – or to complete the Jewish law with some kind of a kingly rule. Jesus did not want to be a king, never has been a king, and never will be a king. To do so would be to compromise the freedom that he loves so much.

Next Sunday, in a million churches around the world, the masses will be sitting in pews and chanting Praise The Lord! How little they know what they are doing. They will not make Jesus a lord by chanting it, but they will continue their servitude to slavery to others who are more than happy to claim to represent Jesus. Lords, like kings, rule. If you think that Jesus is going to yield his freedom of soul to become your lord, think again; but there are many who are willing to be the lord you want. When you chant in the name of Jesus, Praise The Lord, you won't be getting Jesus, but you will be getting a lord.

How did it all go wrong? That is very easy to tell. It went wrong because people have always wanted lords. In fact, people have always demanded lords. How else do you think cruel kingdoms can exist on this earth? Because people want to be ruled. It's easy to be ruled if you want to be ruled. The people in the days of Jesus wanted to be ruled. They wanted Moses to rule them. They wanted David to rule them. They wanted Jesus to rule them. Not Moses, not David, not Jesus could have ruled them except they wanted to be ruled. It was to a world that wanted to be ruled in which Jesus was born.

Jesus – King of the Jews! Why was it written? Because they needed a king. But they did not want the king they had – a Roman king. They wanted their own king. The trouble is they picked on someone to become their king who could not and would not ever become one. Sadly, we are doing the same thing today. Sadly, we still want to be ruled; and sadly, we still think that Jesus will be our king. But Jesus will never be a king – let alone our king. How little we know of Jesus to even begin to suspect that someday he will relent and put a crown on his head so that we as willing subjects can rule over our alleged enemies.

You see, we were not offered the truth about Jesus because those who wrote about him did not know him. They wrote fanciful stories about someone they hoped would be their king someday; and they probably made up a lot of their stories. They could not have an impotent king. So they wrote him as performing powerful miracles and raising dead people to life. But Jesus was not about power. *He was about freedom.* They did not know that then, though; and for the most part, we still do not know it. We are still looking for the same king that they were looking for – but as they never found their king in Jesus, never will anyone.

In *THE GOSPEL ACCORDING TO THOMAS* (Verse 81), Jesus said: *Let him who has power renounce it!* But, you see, you did not get that gospel. Did you? No! That gospel that has Jesus renouncing power was suppressed by the "kings of the day." No king wants to be challenged. Any king worth his salt must offer to the people ideas that lend to control of others. What king would go about telling his subjects that all with power should release it? That would include him – and there would go his kingdom. And what bishop who revels in power would denounce it?

Sadly, people who want power are using Jesus as a claim to power when Jesus was never about power. But people who are caught up with power are unawares of what they are doing. Sincerely, power people think that Jesus was about power because it was a "powerful Jesus" that was given them as a legend. Truly, they expect to rule with Christ in the end. They are not pretending. They are only deceived. But for whatever reason they believe that they will someday become a member of a power Kingdom of Jesus, it can't be. Again, the day that Jesus agrees to be their king just because they want one is the day that Jesus will lose his freedom.

I love Jesus. I find in Jesus a very kindly companion – or in thoughts of Jesus. Jesus said that I should be kind to all. Now you should know why. **Unkindness to one who is unkind only makes two who are unkind; but being unkind is to control.** Tell me how you can possibly be unkind to another and not have him or her in your service or control? The very nature of unkindness, regardless of reason, is to control another. Can you imagine Jesus being unkind to another? If he were unkind, then he would have been in some control of that person. **You cannot be unkind and still be free.**

Is America being unkind to the unkind in the current war in Iraq? Of course it is. So we are controlling Iraq – or trying to control it. What is it getting us? By trying to control it, it is controlling us. When people wake up and realize that putting their energies to any kind of control of others is to lose their freedom, then maybe true freedom will begin to have a chance in this world.

Is President Bush free? Ask him. But President Bush and all those who want power have not an inkling of their jeopardizing their own freedom by wanting the power they do. It does, however, irritate me a tad when power people use my friend, Jesus, to stake their claim to power when my Jesus would have none of it. But if it weren't Jesus that they would use, it would be something else. They only use Jesus because it is convenient. Everyone knows Jesus in America. So you use what people know. Right? Make your claim to power by virtue of what the people expect.

Love one another! They said that Jesus taught that. That makes sense. I think he did; but I also think that the reason Jesus said we should love one another and refrain from any kind of unkindness is because he knew that unkindness impacts and negates freedom. **If I don't love you, then there goes my freedom. It is as simple as that.**

Brother Jesus – not **Lord Jesus!** Jesus will never consent to be your lord – or mine – because to do so, he would lose his freedom. Stop calling him a lord and start calling him a brother; and you will begin to realize why he taught as he did. Realize the reason for what you do; and it will be a lot easier to do it. **Love is easy.** There is nothing hard about it. **It is easy because with it there is no control of another.** You cannot control another and love that other at the same time because true love is letting another pursue his or her own adventure. If you claim to love another and then impose a rule upon him or her, it is not love you have, but domination.

Between us, I do wish that people would stop dominating others in the name of one who refused to dominate others. That is my Jesus – and your Jesus if you will dare to claim freedom for yourself. Jesus was a brother, one like us, not one over us. It is Jesus who said that we should love one another. In *THE GOSPEL OF THOMAS*, it is Jesus who told us to renounce power over others. I think I am in good stead in following the course I do – whether Jesus taught it or not – but knowing why I must love makes it so much easer to do so.

Climax

It was only a few days ago as I write this that we had a Good Friday. Next year at this time, we will celebrate a new Good Friday; and two years from now, a whole lot of us will celebrate another Good Friday – and forty years from now, another Good Friday will be cast in the ongoing drama that started 2,000 years ago. We cannot have an Easter without a Good Friday. Such is the script of the ongoing saga of the tale of man and God divided.

Those who are honest who thought that a crucifixion was needed for an Easter to happen should realize that their Good Friday changed nothing. It was supposed to bring God into our lives and erase the previous division; but it did nothing. God and man are still as divided now as they were when the Mel Gibson directors decided that a Good Friday had to be part of the great play of life and death. They allowed a little room at the end for an Easter, but only a moment – and then it was back to gearing up for next year's Good Friday.

How man loves the idea that he or she is separated from God! The very thought that there is no division and never has been is just too galling to admit. It is just too damned embarrassing to have to admit we were wrong – and so we continue being wrong and we continue looking forward to next year's Good Friday. And we continue living our lives like someday in some great beyond we will finally look up and see God face to face. Oh – that wonderful day! It will have made all the Good Fridays that we had to suffer worth it. Finally – we will be home!

Me? I will erase the Good Fridays from my calendar of years – and I will have only Easter. There is no need for me to suffer in order to drain some kind of misplaced notion of unworthiness from my liver and kidneys and heart and mind and soul. I do not have an unworthy liver. I do not have an unworthy set of kidneys. I do not have an unworthy heart or mind or soul. **All of me is worthy right now.** I do not have to wait beyond some mistaken Good Friday of the future before God and me are finally one. **My God and me are one today!** I can't see his face except in my own and in every other entity – alive and otherwise; but that is saying one heck of a lot. Isn't it?

5

Child of Humanity

5/4/2005

"Peace be with you. Receive my peace. Be careful that no one leads you astray by saying, 'Look here' or 'Look there.' The child of humanity is within you. Follow that. Those who seek it will find it. Go and preach the good news of the Kingdom."

Does the quote above make sense to you? It makes a lot of sense to me; and it is for that reason that I take it to heart. It comes from the 1st verse (of 5) of **THE GOSPEL OF MARY.** It is guessed that the Mary of authorship is Mary Magdalene – a lady who walked with Jesus; however, I do not want to discuss the legitimacy of authorship of the verse – rather just the verse itself. Mary attributes the quote above to Jesus. I tend to believe that Jesus may have said it, but as I look at life now, I look for ideas that may help me appreciate life. In the end, it should not matter if Jesus said it or if George said it or if Harriet said it or if Wilma said it. The question is, regardless of its source, does it make sense?

Let us just say that I think the one who offered the above verse was a sage – a very wise person. In this world of widespread folly, it is always nice to bump into wisdom; and, for me, excellent wisdom just oozes from the above verse.

First of all, the author of the statement claims to be a person of peace. *Receive my peace,* he says. Then before offering us a definition of his peace – or how he may have attained his peace, he offered a warning that we should *be careful that no one leads us astray by saying, 'Look here' or 'Look there.'* That is really the same as telling us that we should watch that others do not tell us that we can find Peace or Salvation over here or over there – in terms of a place. Assuming that the author of this quote is Jesus, and I do believe that is a fair assumption, Jesus is warning us about trying to find Peace in a place – here or there – in the sky or in a forest – or wherever. It – Peace or Paradise - is not in a place. It is in a mysterious image he calls *the child of humanity* within us.

I do not know about you, but - Wow! That is really good news! Jesus offers that we should find the child of humanity within us; and that is the key to finding the peace he offered at the beginning of the verse. *Receive my peace,* he said, and then after warning us that his peace could not be found here or there as in a place or person, it can be found by chasing the *child of humanity* within us.

It becomes, then, as a riddle. Know what the child of humanity within us is, then appraise it and praise it – and presto – Peace. Can it really be as simple as that? Jesus – or the Jesus of Mary – seemed to think it is. So, let us go stalking the child of humanity within us. What could it mean? Jesus did not tell us what it is. So that means if we are to find it, we have to first discover its meaning.

Assuming then, that we are looking for a really simple idea, might we find the meaning of *child of humanity* by transfixing the term to say *humanity as a child.* In other words, we are looking for a *child that is humanity.* That would certainly be simple. Right? Again, we should ask, could it be as simple as that?

What is a child? It is only an offspring. Right? So, let us rephrase our *child of humanity* into *offspring of humanity.* But if humanity is an offspring, of what is it an offspring? In general, I think, we could say *NATURE.* Right? So now we have proceeded to see humanity itself – or the species of humanity – as an offspring of Nature. Now, go find yourself in that – and you have found peace.

In other words, to find peace, stop looking at yourself as only an individual, and start looking at yourself as an image of an entire species. When you do, you become lost in your own humanity. Humanity itself, then, becomes your prime focus – and not just yourself within humanity. Look for the child of Nature that is Humanity within you. This, I think, is what Jesus may have meant when he urged us to find the *child of humanity* within us. **It is to find the child of Nature & God that is humanity within us.**

Now, test that notion for peace. Does it make you peaceful? Does it dress you with a sense of awe? Does it urge a feeling within you that you belong? Of course, you have to answer that question for yourself. It may not lure you into a sense of peace; but it does me. Whenever I think of myself as only one of a wonderful species that we just happen to call **humanity,** I become totally lost within a sense of security. No longer am I merely an individual. **I am now all of humanity.** When I look at myself now, I see first and foremost, a species. After finding the species that is me, then I can identify the me within that species; **but the real key for finding peace is to first locate humanity within you – and then the individual human.**

It takes all the guesswork out of having to deal with life, doesn't it? No longer do you have to measure up to some civilized regimen in order to know your meaning. You can find your meaning simply by looking at your humanity. Never mind all the divisive competition among humans that we humans seem to think belies our meaning. To hell with having to compete with my fellow man. I am now man in general; and what man, in general, has a need to compete with himself – or herself? When I look at me now, I do not see Francis William Bessler at first. I see all of humanity as reflected in me. Francis William Bessler can be reduced to FWB and then to fwb and then to fw and then to f and then – oops – gone! But not only gone – but gone in peace.

Am I really gone? Of course not! I am very much alive – in fact, far more alive than I have ever been before. I do not lose my personality by finding my meaning in belonging to humanity. I merely find my meaning by losing my identity within humanity – and beyond that – within the animal kingdom – and beyond that – **within Nature in General** – and beyond that – **Within God.** I do not stop with my humanity. I only start there; but what a wonderful place to start?

The *good news of the Kingdom,* then, seems to be something entirely different than salvation from Evil. The regular gospels would have us believe that Jesus was all about saving us from some mysterious thing or force called Evil. From the concept of *child of humanity,* I get a very different message. Evil goes away. Evil becomes impertinent. I never have to fear this thing called Evil if I pursue the *child of humanity* within me because I become immune to Evil, if it exists at all. I become immune to Evil because I no longer focus on it. If it exists, I could care less. My focus is now on loving the humanity that is me; and with my new focus, any former obsession disappears. Like Jesus allegedly said elsewhere, Get behind me, Satan! In other words, be gone from my focus and my sight. **Get the hell out of my life – and get hell out of my life!**

Now, go look at yourself in the mirror. Look for humanity and no longer yourself. Look at your husband beside you. He is no longer your husband, but humanity. Look at your wife beside you. She is no longer your wife, but humanity. Look at your child standing there between you. She or he is no longer just a child – but far more importantly – *a child of humanity*. Look at your neighbor. He or she does not exist. Humanity exists in his or her place. By looking at the **humanity child** that is in you and in your neighbor and in every single person on this earth, individuals, though extremely important, go away and humanity itself takes their place.

How can you lose by seeing it that way? How can you not be at peace? Of course, it takes doing it – and not just speculating about it. Nothing is ever ours unless we do it, unless we practice it, unless we live it.

Does God go away with this perspective? It can if you wish I suppose. I don't wish, however; and so God will not go away with this new perspective for me. Humanity itself has to come from something. Doesn't it. Nature itself has to come from something. Doesn't it? Well, for me, that something is God. I don't lose God by asserting my humanity. In fact, I find God in a much more peaceful manner than ever before by declaring to myself that my humanity itself is from and in God. The mystery that is humanity does not become solved with my equation of myself to it. That wonderful mystery still lingers; but I become lost in the mystery without ever needing to resolve it.

So, there it is, my idea of really what the *good news of the Kingdom* that Jesus offered is all about. Kingdom in this sense becomes the **Kingdom of Humanity.** The Kingdom of Nature and the **Kingdom of Humanity** itself is the *good news.* Any government or "kingdom" within humanity becomes mostly unimportant – and any kingdom or government outside of humanity becomes mostly unimportant. Who should care what there is outside of humanity – in terms of assumed greater importance? It is humanity itself that becomes important – and peace is only recognizing that for any of us who are human, humanity itself is the crown jewel. **Despise your humanity; and you will never find peace.**

Does that mean that each human should somehow sacrifice him or herself for the good of some greater humanity? Absolutely not! Humanity is not a god. Humanity is only a species child of God. No one need sacrifice anything for it. Humanity cannot grow because someone thinks he or she owes something to it. Humanity does not depend upon my adoring it. It just is. Humanity is just as much one as it is a billion. It does not depend on numbers. To know one human is to know all of humanity. I do not have to explain it to love it. Peace – the Peace of Jesus – can be attained by respecting humanity as a mysterious **Child of God** – or even merely a **Child of Nature**. I become at peace by recognizing that little bitty me is part of that wonderful mystery we call **humanity.**

Gratefully belonging to humanity and not finding fault with it, I think, is to find and love that mysterious *child of humanity* Jesus talked about in regard to peace. Pretty simple, huh? And yet many of us have grown up accepting that Jesus taught that he wanted to save us from our humanity – our lovely humanity - because Satan made it evil. How utterly and absurdly Anti-Christ that turns out to be. **Jesus could not have considered humanity Satanic or evil – or he would have never suggested that we pursue it to find peace. Could he have?**

If we are souls that are visiting humanity and then leave to possess some other kingdom somewhere, then, fine, then that new kingdom becomes the important kingdom – but for the same reason that humanity itself was a kingdom for us. In it, we can lose ourselves; and in it, we can find God – for no matter what the kingdom of which we may be part – human, animal, or maybe, angelic – being the ultimate source of all things, God always remains the Grandfather or Grandmother of all that is. In loving the kingdom in which we reside, how can we not be loving God – the ultimate source of that kingdom?

And if we do not love the kingdom in which we reside, peace will always be absent; for how can anyone attain peace if he or she considers war with a kingdom of residence proper? Again, Jesus would not recommend being at war with our membership within humanity because he urged us to love our humanity. *Look for the child of humanity within you,* he said, and *follow that. Those who seek it will find it. Go and preach the good news of the Kingdom* – **The Kingdom of Humanity.**

Are we listening?

The Key For Finding Peace

Recitation with Refrain
by
Francis William Bessler
May, 2005

REFRAIN:
What is the key for finding peace –
if you're human like me?
Well, Jesus told us long ago –
if peace we should like to know,
we can find it if we seek
within us – the child of humanity.

A long time ago, Jesus said –
please receive my peace;
but don't be led astray
by those who know it not.
If someone says it's here or there –
or beyond where you can see,
do not be fooled.
I'll tell you how it should be sought.
Refrain.

Then Jesus said, listen to me –
I'll share with you my ways.
It is not near as hard
as you may think it is.
You cannot find peace by looking
in that which rusts or decays.
Look within your image –
to find that which has no sin.
Refrain.

Jesus then continued to tell –
look for the child of humanity,
but do not look for it
only in someone else.
The child of humanity is within you
and can make you free
if you'll just look at it –
and find an image of yourself.
Refrain.

Then Jesus said, listen here –
I'll tell you of my good news,
but the idea doesn't
just belong to me.
For anyone who is human,
humanity itself is the truth
For everything is from God –
in your image, find Divinity.
Refrain.

So, let us, one and all –
preach the good news of the Kingdom,
realizing it has always
been within our reach.
The good news of the Kingdom
is that we are equally human.
If peace is what we want –
only that can we teach.
Refrain.

6

Freedom

5/23/2005

"Peace be with you. Receive my peace. Be careful that no one leads you astray by saying, 'Look here' or 'Look there.' The child of humanity is within you. Follow that. Those who seek it will find it. Go and preach the good news of the Kingdom. Do not lay down any rules other than what I have given you, and do not establish law as the lawgiver did, or you will be bound by it. When he said this, he left them."

My last article was on the ***Child of Humanity*** that Jesus offered that we should seek within in order to find peace. It was my determination that the *child of humanity* that Jesus suggested we follow as the **only rule** necessary to find peace is really nothing more than **humanity as a child.** Humanity itself takes on a new special importance – as if it should be our main focus while we live as souls within it. That makes a lot of sense to me because I see my soul as occupying a human vessel for its usefulness. So why should I go through life ignoring the humanity I chose when incarnating into this world? While I am here, I should not only revere humanity itself, but love the human that is in me.

This month, I am talking about **freedom** as related to the goal of peace. We have determined what we should do to find peace. Now, let us pursue freedom through that concept. Though it is almost never presented as such, I think that the very best definition of **Freedom** is **Peace**. For me, the two are interchangeable. Freedom is Peace and Peace is Freedom. Why? Because being free for me is only feeling content with my life. To the degree that I do not sense contentment, I lack freedom. It may be something other than that for others, but **freedom and peace equals contentment** for me.

I think it was that way for Jesus too. I think Jesus saw himself as free because he knew himself as content. When one is content, one is merely satisfied with one-self – without relating to others. If my satisfaction is dependent upon my relationship to others, then I will never be free because I will never be content. Keep in mind that we are all human. **To respect the humanity in one should be to respect the humanity in all.** Thus, by merely isolating myself as my own representative of humanity, I can honor the *child of humanity* or humanity itself strictly through me.

I repeated the initial part of the 1st Verse of *THE GOSPEL OF MARY* that I offered in the last article because I think it establishes the true nature of freedom.

It is looking for something within me without having to look toward someone else to find it. That is the real essence of freedom. The opposite of freedom, then, would be having to depend upon a relationship with another to become satisfied with life. The more we depend on others outside ourselves for our content-ment with life, the more we lack true freedom. Finding peace through self-contentment is the true essence of freedom. If that is so, then finding peace or freedom by dependency on others becomes the antithesis of freedom and peace.

In the last article about finding the *Child of Humanity* within me, I did not include the remainder of the verse about the theme, but I think that conclusion is due now. How did the Jesus of Mary say it? *Do not lay down any rules other than what I have given you, and do not establish law as the lawgiver did, or you will be bound by it.*

Would you not agree that translates into law being the very antithesis of freedom and peace. Why? Because law is bound within relationships. It stands to reason, then, that if peace and freedom cannot be achieved except through self-contentment, attention to satisfac-tion through others and essentially, law, becomes the greatest obstacle to freedom.

I am so pleased that a **Gospel of Mary** was found because it just so happens to state my case very well. Law is the very antithesis of freedom and peace because it conditions its results on the cooperation of many. Some degree of satisfaction may result from the cooperation of many, but the cooperation of many can never lead to the ideal of peace and freedom.

The Jesus I know offered this warning against law and not the message he has been accused of offering – that peace and contentment can only be had through him as a needed personal savior. Jesus insisted on each of us depending upon ourselves for any virtue we might attain – and not what he has been accused of insisting – that we must depend on him for our virtue. Jesus insisted that we ignore any law of old that purports to be a requirement for salvation – and not what he has been accused of advocating – that old law can only be perfected with new law.

Old law/new law was out for Jesus because he knew full well that any law cannot assure self contentment. Law by its very nature is two or more oriented. Peace and/or freedom by its very nature is solitary oriented. It only takes one to be free, but where there are two or more by requirement, law sneaks in and destroys freedom. When two must relate to find peace and contentment, then conditions are interjected into the picture; and wherever there is a condition, there can be no freedom.

Do not establish law, as the lawgiver did, or you will be bound by it. Perhaps it is different with you, but being bound by any rule that I cannot find within myself is not my idea of freedom. I am free only to the degree that I am independent of you, not dependent upon you. We make law to regulate ourselves because we think that intelligent beings must do that, but the laws we make bind us to one another and prevent freedom. That is what Jesus knew; and yet the traditional churches of Jesus have offered the exact opposite of that – that the way to peace and freedom is paved with law and restriction. How often have we heard? Narrow is the way to salvation, but wide is the way to perdition. Thus we have seen fit to make of Jesus a lawgiver whom we must obey or suffer eternal damnation by another – amazingly, by Jesus himself as the "Son" of a very judgmental God. Jesus a lawgiver? Nothing could be further from the truth.

When I listen to the **rule** of finding the **Child of Humanity** within me as the only moral guide needed for my soul, then any law is not only useless, but necessarily obstructive. If I have to pay attention to something other than loving the child of humanity within me, then loving the child of humanity within me becomes insufficient. I suppose there are many who think it is insufficient, but having lived the notion, I think, I find it indeed sufficient. Moral laws exist all around me, of course, but having decided that no law is necessary, I ignore them all. Thus, as Jesus would argue, I am not bound by them either.

In reality, you can only be morally bound by something you say yes to. If you agree that some law is needed, then you are bound to it – and bound by it. I am speaking morally now – not civilly. There is no question I should obey all civil rules laid down by man for the greater security of society – or pay the price for disobedience by imprisonment or fine at the very least. Civil law should not be construed as equivalent to moral law. Moral law is that law which is imposed on me for the safety of my soul – not my body or person. It is not my argument that I do not have to obey civil laws. It is only my argument that if I choose some moral law to guide me and restrict me, then I am automatically constrained within that law – or laws.

Recently, I read a fascinating book dealing with the existence of an astral world – or perhaps astral worlds. I need not go into details, but essentially there may be many expressions within the astral world – or spiritual world – that reflect the many different options of soulful obedience. Theoretically, there are many different layers of what could be called consciousness within the astral world. Regardless of it being called an "astral world" or "spiritual world" or "consciousness world" or whatever, I do think it makes sense that each so called "level" is comprised of souls who command themselves according to some spiritual regimen.

If I agree to submit to any norm of obedience, then I am – de facto – part of that norm. In the way that Jesus may have said it, I am bound by the laws to which I agree. You might have a level 1 in the astral or spiritual world of belief in and attention to Christian Law. You might have a level 2 in the astral world of belief in and attention to Judaic Law. You might have a level 3 in the astral world of belief in and attention to Islamic Law. And perhaps levels 4 through 9 represent some other established regimen of behavior. Then on a level 10 are those who pay no attention to any law, but are safely secure within the notion of *Child of Humanity*.

Does that not make sense? Isn't that the way it would likely work? Isn't that the way it would likely work in a so called spiritual realm because that is exactly the way it works within a civil realm? I do not choose Chinese Law – whatever that is – and therefore, I am not bound by it. I do not choose Islamic Law – whatever that is – and therefore, I am not bound by it. I do not choose Judaic Law – whatever that is – and therefore, I am not bound by it. I do not choose traditional Christian Law – whatever that is – and therefore, I am not bound by it. All of those laws oblige others who recognize them; but they do not oblige me because, in essence, I am outside of them. I am restricted by no law – only by one rule – **to love the humanity (or humanity child) within me.**

Should I not love that child, then it is only love that I lack. Having given myself to no law, I am bound by none of it. This is what is so terribly important about the Jesus we have missed. He knew this – and he taught this, if we are believe in *THE GOSPEL OF MARY*. I think that the regular gospel writers of the *BIBLE* – if you want to call them that – did not understand the most crucial of issues that Jesus tried to teach. He tried to teach that no law is useful to the soul that wants to find peace and freedom because all law is many oriented. Old law – no good! New law – no good! And yet, very sincerely, Peter and Paul and all their partners mistook Jesus as a lawgiver. Jesus could not have been about any law and still have been about freedom because freedom, by nature, is only solitary oriented.

In Verse 75 of *THE GOSPEL OF THOMAS, Jesus said: Many are standing at the door, but the solitary are the ones who will enter the bridal chamber.* Why would he say a thing like that? Because he was trying to tell us that laws regarding two or more are absolutely worthless in the search for peace and contentment and freedom. If you do not find it within, you will never find it in another – even if that other is Jesus himself. That was the Jesus that was – not that lord the others proclaimed as a new law directing to a new heaven. Law, in general, is about as **Anti-Christ** as you can get. Those who obey will automatically be bound within it; but freedom will never be the result.

In Verse 70 of *THE GOSPEL OF THOMAS, Jesus said: If you bring forth that within yourselves, that which you have will save you. If you do not have that within yourselves, that which you do not have within you will kill you.* Again, the now totally logical emphasis on find meaning within yourselves because you can never find it in anyone else – given that you are trying to find something in another that is not in yourself. That is the only way that moral law makes sense – that my meaning cannot be found within myself alone, as representative of all things natural and divine. If I see myself as inadequate, I will live life that way; and I will be bound to the lords of all worlds of law to which I yield.

So, what is freedom? It is really obedience to a single rule – that whatever is in me is all that is needed for virtue. I am free to be complete in me. I need no one else because all they are, I am. If I need something in you that is not also in me, then I am not sufficient. The Jesus of Thomas and Mary would not agree. If I have to depend on you for virtue that is actually found in me, then if you withdraw from me, even though the virtue I want is in me, that which I do not realize is in me will kill me. Why? Because that is my mind frame; and when it all comes down to it, each of us is obligated to the rules or laws of our mind – not to the rules or laws of anyone else. I am talking spiritually now – not civilly. As we believe it – so it is; but as we cooperate with others in the same belief, that becomes our community.

That is probably how it works in the spiritual world because that is how it works in the civil world. With those with whom we join hands in some common agreement, they become our community. It probably works that way because God is equally in everyone. So, community cannot be defined related to the presence of God since every community has an equal presence of God. We are not separated in life by virtue of a different presence of God. We are separated by virtue of a different vision of God perhaps, but not by any real different presence of God. Our vision of God may well play a part in the laws we make for ourselves, but regardless of reason for law, in the end, we will only be bound together – or freed together – by a common bond of belief.

In Verse 5 of *THE GOSPEL OF THOMAS, Jesus said: Know what is in thy sight, and what is hidden from thee will be revealed to thee. For there is nothing hidden that will not be manifest.* Relating this to law, how does it apply? In the world that I can see, I note bunches of people relating to and obeying an Islamic Law – and presto, they are being bound within it. Others who are Christian are not being bound by those laws. Are they? In the world that I can see, I note bunches of people relating to and obeying Christian Law – and presto, they are being bound within it. Others who are Moslem are not being bound by those laws. Are they? In the world that I can see, I note bunches of people relating to and obeying what might be called a Buddhist regimen. Others who are Moslem and Christian do not feel themselves obligated to such a regimen. Right?

So there it is. *Know what is in thy sight, and what is hidden from thee will be revealed to thee.* There in front of us is the evidence. People are bound by the laws they choose for themselves; but others outside a regimen are not bound by the laws others choose. And Jesus and me and hopefully you – we are bound only by loving the *child of humanity* within us. Wonderfully, that frees us from having to attend any of the laws that bind.

Why does it work that way? Because there are lords who make it happen. Keep in mind that law is socially oriented. That means that laws are made by some who expect others to obey. When I give myself to a law, I give myself to the lords of that law. Thus, those lords and their lieutenants will stand by to enforce their law. That is the sad part of it. If I give myself to any law – made by some lord or other – then I will see myself as having to account for myself in front of that lord. It matters not who the lord is. It only matters that I think I am obligated to obey him.

This probably does not change when we die. The same lords who invisibly contracted us to obedience while we were in the body will be standing about to receive us when we leave the body. Amazingly, we may not even know there has been a change from one world to the next. We will expect to see lords; and they will gladly oblige. That is probably the way it works after death because that is exactly the way it works before death. Isn't it? And make no mistake about it. For those of us expecting to see a Mohammed as lord, we will see one, though it may not be Mohammed himself – but an impostor. For those of us expecting to see a Jesus as lord, we will see one, though it may not be Jesus himself – but an impostor. We will know no different, though. **People realize what they expect.** It will not even occur to a Jesus fan that it is not Jesus standing there, bidding him or her to more obedience; and the blind soul will continue to bow and serve. To each, his or her own, but that is not my idea of freedom.

When he said this, he left them. That is how the 1st Verse of *THE GOSPEL OF MARY* ends. The "he" of reference, of course, is Jesus. Where did he go? Who knows? Did he stick around to be crucified? I think there is a good chance that was his ending, but that is the story the others told. They looked upon Jesus as a lord. They acted like Jesus was a lord; and they may have fabricated a suitable ending for a lord. I do not know about that; but assuming that Jesus was crucified, that fits in well with my image of him as one who preached self-esteem.

You see, for one who depends only on his or her self-esteem, nothing anyone else does or does not do can infringe upon one's freedom. Death is an illusion in a way. For the soul, it does not really happen; but one with true self-esteem cannot be affected by death. No one can harm your soul but you; though there is plenty of harm that one can do to oneself – just by virtue of one's beliefs.

As you believe, so it is for you – be it in this life or the next. If Jesus had lashed out at his persecutors, he would have demonstrated an anger and not a peace; and anger stems from dissatisfaction with others; but Jesus did not lash out because he was happy with himself; and happiness with self always overrides any dissatisfaction with others. For me, the crucifixion of Jesus – though admittedly it may not have actually happened – only climaxed a story of true freedom. In life, Jesus was free. Through death, Jesus remained free; and so will any of us who loved the freedom that Jesus loved.

Consider it the greatest of all moral rules. It is not a law – but a rule. No one will punish you if you fail it. You will only punish yourself. What is that rule? **Be happy with what you are.** Many violate that rule and go searching for an excuse in some fashion of law or power that extends outside themselves. They want law to make it right; but whatever the law that might seem to override it, no law really ever does. They want power over others to show themselves that they do not have to be satisfied with themselves; but inevitably, the powerful reflect their true impotence because happiness was never seeded in power to make over either oneself or another, but with contentment with oneself.

If I am happy with what I am, regardless of the dimensions, then I can change those dimensions and still retain the happiness; but if I am unhappy with what I am and change the dimensions to make myself happy with a new me, in time, the new me will become as the old me and a new make over will be needed. If you want to change yourself, first make sure you are happy with what you are, and then you can change yourself to your heart's content and love every form that results; but if you begin with self-dissatisfaction, you will always end with it. You will always find a reason to be unhappy.

Looking For A New Me

By
Francis William Bessler
May, 2005

REFRAIN:
I am looking for a new me, but where will I find it.
I am looking for a new me, but where will it be?
I am looking for a new me, but how shall I find it
If I don't begin being happy with me.

Some look at life like a field of power
with others to serve them as their slaves.
They have no meaning all by themselves
and their favorite word in life is "estate."

I look at life like a garden of flowers
with maybe some weeds thrown in too.
Regardless what it is, everything's still a plant
and every plant has it own beauty to view.
Refrain (2).

Some look at life like they must improve
the nature they find that's so full of sin.
They do not like the lives that they have
and they measure all by a sprint or a win.

I look at life like an opportunity to find –
to find my own soul in a body of flesh.
Others are nice, but are not important.
All I need is in me, my soul to refresh.
Refrain (2).

It doesn't seem to me hard to understand
the key to happiness is a thing called pride.
If you have it now, you will have it later -
and what's in yourself cannot be denied.

I look at life like everything's perfect
and that change is only enjoying it all.
As long as I love everything I am,
I can change completely and still be enthralled.
Refrain (3).

7

Independence

7/3/2005

Would it be more correct to say – poor, poor Jesus for our tragic misunderstanding of him – or **poor, poor us**? If anyone answered that question by saying it is more correct to say poor, poor Jesus – in my opinion, they have a very poor understanding of Jesus; and if anyone answered that question by saying neither response is correct because Jesus was not misunderstood, well, to each, his or her own, but anyone who doesn't believe that Jesus was misunderstood, to put it bluntly, such a one is **far from the Kingdom;** but it is us that are poor for the misunderstanding – not Jesus – because in our misunderstanding, it is like we walk right by Paradise everyday without ever setting foot inside it.

Why is there so much violence in the world? Why is so much of the violence of the world tied to Christians who have been clearly taught that Jesus championed kindness and forgiveness at all costs? Why have there been conquistadores down through history all the way to the current day who have marched and plundered and killed in the name of Jesus? Why? **Because Jesus was misunderstood.**

Personally, I think the basis of that misunderstanding is a false connection of Jesus to the **Old Testament**. Even today, many so called Christian services drop back to the **Old Testament** to get a predating of Jesus. They are convinced that Jesus came from the **Old Testament** like Moses came from Mount Sinai. Moses did not come from Mount Sinai originally, however. He only visited there; and Jesus never came from the **Old Testament** – though he, too, may have visited there with some of his teachings.

In truth, you cannot find Moses on Mount Sinai because he existed as he was before he went up the mountain; and you cannot find Jesus in the **Old Testament** because his living had nothing to do with all the unholy blunders that are depicted in those works. I think the biggest reason we have misunderstood Jesus is that we have tied him to the **Old Testament** and therefore, expect a certain sanctification of **Old Testament** ways in the process.

Where does an eye for an eye and a tooth for a tooth come from? Of course, the **Old Testament**. Where does thy enemies are my enemies come from? Of course, the **Old Testament**. Where does God hates the evil doer come from? Of course, the **Old Testament**. On and on and on, it goes. The sad thing is that most folks who think they know Jesus are absolutely sure that Jesus has no meaning outside the **Old Testament**. The **Old**

Testament prophesied Jesus; and Jesus had no meaning except to fulfill those prophecies.

How many times is it pronounced in the **New Testament** that such and such happened to Jesus *in order to fulfill the prophecies of old?* Jesus was born of a virgin *in order to fulfill the prophecies of old.* Jesus was three days in a tomb between death and resurrection because it was necessary *to fulfill the prophecies.* Jesus was taken down from the cross before the normal expenditure time of criminals crucified because it was necessary *to fulfill the prophecies.* Remember – Jesus was three days in the earth like Jonah was three days in the belly of a whale. All this constant tying of Jesus to the **Old Testament** is, I think, the biggest reason we have misunderstood him.

If God can hate, so can we. That is the general lesson we get by tying the **Old Testament** to the **New Testament.** Never mind that God can't hate; and the **Old Testament** is flat out wrong about that and a million other things. What is hatred? **It is wanting to deny another life.** Can God hate? Can God Who or Which makes us all want to deny us life after He or She or It has gone to the trouble of creating us? The **Old Testament** constantly affirms that God can hate when nothing could be further from the truth.

Why do conquistadores act like murder in the name of God is OK? Why? Because the **Old Testament** condones it; and if the **Old Testament** condones execution in the name of God, then if Jesus is the fulfillment of the **Old Testament**, then Jesus, too, must condone righteous execution of God's enemies. Never mind that it is clear that he taught that just thinking about murder is to murder. Never mind that it is clear that he taught kindness to all – including one's enemies – is the first and only commandment necessary for a soul. Never mind that it is clear that he taught that each of us must forgive the other *seven times seventy times.* Never mind all that. Look there! Can you see it? Moses and Jesus coming down from Mount Sinai hand in hand with each patting the other on the back and with each justifying what the other has proclaimed.

What that has done is Kill the Independence of Jesus; and with the death of the true independence of Jesus, every one of us who have been taught about Jesus have been misled. Sadly, for those of us who have a liking for Jesus – and I admit to be in the vast number of those who qualify – by Jesus losing his independence from the **Old Testament**, we who are his students have lost our independence as well.

Many, of course, think that Jesus did not want independence from the **Old Testament** and did not want us – his students to be independent of either the **Old Testament** or him; but I sense a different story. I detect a Jesus who believed in independence of the individual upon anyone outside the individual for a sense of worth. It is my reading of Jesus – especially via the **Gospels of Thomas and Mary** – that primary for Jesus for himself and for his students was and is a state of independence. I think the real Jesus taught that we all have intrinsic worth because, as he would offer it, we are *sons (or children) of the Living Father.* Being sons of the Living Father – or God – we are exactly as we should be. Our problems in this world is that we do not believe we are really *sons of the Living Father.*

In Verse 3 of *THE GOSPEL OF THOMAS, Jesus said: If those who lead you say to you: "See, the Kingdom is in heaven, then the birds of the heaven will precede you. If they say to you: "It is in the sea," then the fish will precede you. But the Kingdom is within you and it is without you. If you will know yourselves, then you will be known and you will know that you are the sons of the Living Father. But if you do not know yourselves, then you are in poverty and you are poverty.* For me, this is the real Jesus – teaching me that I am fine as I am. He did not say I am only fine with him. He said I am right now a *son of the Living Father.* Right now, the Kingdom is within me. It is not a future thing. It is a right now thing.

Where do you see in the above quote any need whatsoever to be instructed in the **Old Testament**? Where in the above quote is there any sense of intrinsic sin within me – or you? Where in the above quote can you find anything but a sense of individual worth without any need of any additional grace to fulfill me – or you? He is telling us that we already have the Kingdom within us; yet the **Old Testament** & the **New Testament** pretend that we are evil to the core and need some additional grace to make us complete. The Jesus of Thomas or Mary does not say that. The quote above tells me that Jesus is offering that if I really know myself, I should be very much aware that I am a *son of the Living Father.*

I do not know about you, but that is news for rejoicing. Why should I hang my head after hearing such good news and pretend that I am not a *son of the Living*

Father just as I am? I am not making myself. The Living Father is. This Jesus of Thomas (and Mary) is not suggesting that I need him for a sense of worth. In fact, he is saying just the opposite. I am now – right now – the son I should be. I do not need a makeover; and anyone who thinks I do need a makeover is listening to a false Jesus. I am independently holy – right now – because I am right now a *son of the Living Father.* I do not need redeemed. I have never become estranged from God. The **Old Testament** teaches that I have become estranged from God, but the Jesus of Thomas is telling me – in essence – the **Old Testament** is wrong.

I am sure I have offered elsewhere in these essays that Jesus tried to divorce himself from the **Old Testament**. In Verse 52 of *THE GOSPEL OF THOMAS, His disciples said to Him: Twenty four prophets spoke in Israel and they all spoke about Thee. He said to them: You have dismissed the Living One who is before you and you have spoken about the dead.* That is to say, I think, please do not crowd me in with all those dead prophets of the **Old Testament** because if you do, you will be dismissing me for the Independent One I am.

Why didn't they recognize him for the independent one he was? Number 1, because they did not want independence from the **Old Testament** and number 2, because they did not want independence from the world. In truth, no one can recognize independence unless they want independence. Why couldn't the so called disciples of Jesus see him for what he was? Because they wanted him otherwise. They wanted him to fulfill a role of promised messiah; and for that reason, they could not recognize him for who he really was. Likewise, all of those who insist on needing Jesus as some kind of personal savior blot him out as anything other than messiah. They are not interested in Jesus except that he is the completion of the **Old Testament**; and so, like all the blind Jews of the days of Jesus on earth, they will continue to see only what they want.

When I see you, what do I see? I see a *son (or daughter) of the Living Father.* Because I see you as such, without the need for any additional grace, I also see you naked. I see you naked because I see you as whole without need of additional ornament to make you acceptable. You are acceptable as you are. Nakedness is not primarily a sexual thing for me. It is primarily a worth thing for me. If I am a *living son of the Living Father,* then I am good just as I am – and you are good just as you are.

In Verse 37 of *THE GOSPEL OF THOMAS, His disciples said: When wilt Thou be revealed to us and when will we see Thee? Jesus said: When you take off your clothing without being ashamed, and take your clothes and put them under your feet as the little children and tread on them, then shall you behold the Son of the Living One and you shall not fear.* In this verse, Jesus is telling us that we can not see him as the person he really is unless we can embrace our nakedness without shame. That is certainly not a message we receive in the regular gospels, is it?

To be honest, all my life I have loved nakedness because I have loved independence from evil. Evil – all evil – begins with a downplay of life. **Evil happens when we do not love what we see.** That which we do not want to see we banish; and banishment is a result of seeing evil. Sadly we can see evil where there is none and therefore banish what we should not. I have long refused to banish my life because I have seen such a refusal as being tantamount to admitting imperfection where there is none. I see myself as perfect – not from a worldly point of view, but from a human point of view. I am as perfect as I can be in terms of my humanity.

In the quote above, Jesus at least implied that he was comfortable with his own nakedness and that we should follow suit and be comfortable with ours as well. Did Jesus pounce on Mary Magdalene when he was naked? Of course not. Even if Mary was naked with him, the Jesus I know and try to practice would not engage her in any act resulting in dependency – with the one exception of natural conception. If Jesus agreed with Mary to conceive a child, of course, he would allow female dependency on him to allow her to get pregnant, but outside of that, I doubt it.

My argument here is that I think Jesus approved of nakedness for its being virtuous of itself – not for its advantage of sex. Perhaps it is only a mindset, but it is the mindset I have had all my life – or at least, most of my life. When people tell me that nakedness for the sake of virtue is unrealistic, I want to tell them that unrealistic or not, it has been my own reality. Maybe it is unrealistic for the common herd; but for those of us intent on achieving the greatest of personal virtue we can achieve in life, it is far from unrealistic. In fact, for us, sexual dependency is the most unrealistic of all conduct because it makes of true independence of soul nothing but a hope or a wish.

Poor, poor Jesus – for being misunderstood? No! Jesus is not poor because we have been given a false image of him. We are poor for having believed the false image we have been given. The traditionally understood Jesus has not yielded us the independence from the **Old Testament** he wanted us to have. The **Old Testament** was not banned as Jesus would have wanted; and consequently, our lives remain as jumbled and distorted as they were within the hands of the old prophets. Jesus wanted us to follow him – not the **Old Testament;** but we did not understand him. Thus, we think it is Christian to act as conquistadores and to live in dependence on some additional grace we have been led to call The Holy Spirit.

Poor, poor Jesus? No! **Poor, poor us** for even suspecting that a Holy Spirit is needed to turn us into a *son of the Living Father* when all along we have had independent worth because all along, God – *our Living Father* – has been in us. **What a wonderful mystery we have been all along! What a wonderful mystery we are! And what a wonderful mystery we will always be!**

I Believe In Independence

By
Francis William Bessler
June, 2005

I believe in independence,
especially from law.
I believe in independence,
starting with my thoughts.
I believe in independence
because we are all the same.
All you have I do too.
So, let us celebrate our fame.

People think they need one another
for that which they lack,
but in truth, no one lacks
that which all others have.
It is a game people of power play
to get us to agree
to join with them in some ploy
and give up being free.

Just look at the lonely and see
how they complain when alone.
That's because they pay no attention
to the beauty that they own.
No one is an island.
We all share the same humanity.
There is nothing that you have
that is not also found in me.

It is also the very same way
for each of our souls.
We are the same and all have
to attend the same rules
but the rule of the soul is
that each should be free
of other souls who try to control
and refuse them liberty.

Souls are born into bodies
to practice what they believe.
The body is only a lab
by which we can use to see –
to see what we might be doing
to other souls if we could.
The wise soul will not treat self or others
as a piece of wood.

Wood is something that humans use
to build and to mold,
but it is dead, not alive,
unlike a soul created to be bold.
When people use others as if
they were only blocks of stone,
then light turns to darkness
and souls in their bodies moan.

So, let us one and all,
pledge to see ourselves as whole,
having all the beauty of our Creator
in ourselves alone.
Let us know of our true worth
and then let us all commence
to never let others keep us
from loving our independence.

I believe in independence,
especially from law.
I believe in independence,
starting with my thoughts.
I believe in independence
because we are all the same.
All you have I do too.
So, let us celebrate our fame.

8

Perfection

7/31/2005

Nobody's perfect! That is a statement and philosophy of life to which I do not subscribe. I consider the opposite to be true: *Everybody's perfect.* I think too many souls are caught up with imperfection when they should be focused on perfection. Anyone can find a flaw if he or she insists on finding one; but the mature soul does not go through life finding flaws. The mature soul goes through life being grateful for whatever gift of life with which one has been blessed. Every aspect of life should be considered a blessing. So why go through life pining so called missing blessings when time would be so much better spent being grateful for the blessings you do have?

What is perfect? In my opinion – everything. Everything is perfect because Nature is perfect; and Nature is perfect because it is of God – or God is in it – however you want to look at it. We look at two forms in

Nature and two forms may look alike, but no two forms are exactly alike. Perfection, then, may involve similarity, but never identical expression. All things in Nature vary. That's just the way it is. Perfection for a soul, then, is accepting it the way it is, assuming quite properly that the Master, Nature, is in proper command.

If I have but one eye, I should look at my life like everyone has but one eye and be happy with the one eye I have. If I have but one leg, I should look at my life like everyone has but one leg. If I have but one arm, I should look at my life like everyone has but one arm. Why do different? Anyone can find a flaw if they seek one; but in Nature, there is no such thing as a flaw. I can have one green eye and one brown eye and consider myself imperfect because my condition is out of the ordinary. I can have two wonderful breasts but one is a little smaller than the other and I could consider myself imperfect because my two breasts are not equal.

Anyone can find a flaw and consider themselves imperfect because of it; but the truly mature soul does not look for flaws and realizes variation is not flaw. The mature soul looks at whatever one is and is grateful for the blessing. To do otherwise leads to sickness of soul and that often translates into sickness of body. We can always make ourselves sick just by insisting on finding flaws in life; though for Nature itself, there is no such thing as a flaw. There is only variation. If flaws are our focus, however, if they do not exist before we look for them, they are likely to appear because we expect them. The key is to be content with what you have and focus on what you do have – not pine what you think you lack – be it something in yourself or a companion.

Several years ago, Tom Hanks starred in a movie called **CASTAWAY**. I believe I am correct with that title. It was all about some lad who went down in a great ocean as a passenger of a small airplane. All the crew was lost, but the Tom Hanks character managed to survive and find a nearby island. Much of the rest of the movie was about a forlorn character pining his loneliness and isolation from the rest of the world. He was there for years, but always dreaming about some-one finding him and rescuing him. Eventually, he does make a wooden raft from tree wood on the island and floats out to sea and after days of drifting on the open sea, he is finally rescued by a cargo ship.

It was a very good story. I loved it, but I could not help but wish the story had been written allowing the character to fall in love with himself and his small world. Instead, this script had him always dreaming and planning about rescue. In real life, if a person is so occupied, all he will be is unhappy; but it never has to be that way. If it had been me on that island, chances are good I would have never looked for a way to get off of it – unless I thought I was in danger by staying; but in this story, the island was unoccupied by beast and was very friendly – lots of sunshine and lots of fish and coconuts to eat – and probably a lot of other tasty things too; but the Tom Hanks character pined for being back in civilization and, in my opinion, blew a tremendous opportunity to find completion in himself. He considered his life a flaw without another to share it with him.

If it had been me, I would not have spent a day with clothes. Having the great opportunity I had, I would have wanted to merge with my surroundings. For Heaven's sake, why not? I would not have done what the Tom Hanks character did and "pretend" that I was a civilization of one. Not once that I know of did the movie show Hanks even swimming naked in the ocean. I cannot imagine my swimming in any other way – even if people are around.

I have long felt that the greatest mistake that men and women of humankind make is to insist that we are somehow "different" from the rest of nature and then pride ourselves on being different. As far as I can see, I am not in any meaningful way different than the rest of nature. So, why in the world should I pretend to be?

That is not to say I should not love variety. It is, in fact, a love of variety that should allow me to enjoy being a one armed or one legged or one eyed human among other humans who have two of each. For a mature society of souls caught up with a variety of individual perfections, it should not matter that one among us has one arm or one leg or one eye. What difference should it make? If I am happy with what I am, why should I insist that you must be just like me for me to associate with you? Why can't I embrace you for your own perfection, unique perhaps, but as definite as my own in whatever way I am also perfect?

In *THE GOSPEL OF MARY*, Jesus says: *be of good courage. And if you are discouraged, be encouraged in the presence of the diversity of forms in Nature.* Diversity does not just include the so called "normal." It should also embrace the abnormal as if the abnormal is normal. If we would only do that in this world and not insist that each of us must be just like the other, we could revel in our variety and fall in love with the total world in which we find ourselves. Regardless of what form any of us assumes for the gift of life bestowed upon us, each of us should see our individual form as perfect, not imperfect.

My vision of Jesus is that he was like that too. I see him as a man who valued the solitary, but his solitude was knowing and acting like he is one with Nature and God. Jesus did not look for flaws within his body because he viewed his body as being one with Nature and God. Jesus did not stand alone all by himself. I think he stood with Nature and God – as if he were part of them; and as Jesus acted, we should too.

In the 78th Verse of *THE GOSPEL OF THOMAS, Jesus said: Why did you come out into the desert? To see a reed shaken by the wind? And to see a man clothed in soft garments? Your kings and your great ones are those who are clothed in soft garments and they shall not be able to know the truth.* This verse suggests to me that if Jesus had been the Tom Hanks character on that island, he would not have been found "clothed in soft garments." Like the Tom Hanks character, Jesus was alone in the desert as the Hanks character was alone on an island. Jesus did not pine about being away from civilization and found himself enthralled with being with God and Nature – and for that he had no use for clothes. Why would he? He offers that in the world our kings and great ones are the ones who are dressed in soft garments and almost for that reason, they can not know the truth.

I think that is true. I think that when we close ourselves off from God and Nature, insisting that we are flaws of both God and Nature and insisting on our being "different" from the rest of nature, we automatically close ourselves to wisdom because true wisdom is not noting how different we are, but how much alike we are – even as we revel in our variety as well.

I know my Jesus is not the ordinary Jesus. I realize that many who think that Jesus was primarily socially oriented would not agree with my impression of him as one who would have been found naked in the desert or naked on an isolated island or even naked in a crowd; but my impression of Jesus is what I have found in the Gospels of Thomas and Mary. It is that Jesus that has been the content of these articles and not the Jesus of the Jews of the regular gospels.

In the end, we must all choose the Jesus we believe in – if we find Jesus interesting at all. The Tom Hanks character in **CASTAWAY** should have had copies of the Gospels of Thomas and Mary with him on that island in the Pacific when he was marooned there. If he had, he would still be there, pondering his meaning as a single person and a single soul – and not wandering the streets of Memphis "back from the dead" and choosing to walk among the living dead in search for meaning outside themselves.

9

Conclusion:

Was Jesus

Holistic or Messianic?

I began this series with a mini discussion about what we may have lost when Constantine closed down the avenues of the gospels. With the onset of Constantine as Emperor of the Western World in the 4th Century, many gospels were banned. Some of those banned gospels have somehow survived their condemnation. It seems that now in the 21st Century, we are being allowed to continue the discussion about Jesus that was interrupted so long ago.

Looking at the opinions about life and Jesus like a pie of varying sections and varying content, perhaps one could look at that pie as being one half of one ingredient and the other half of being of another ingredient. When Constantine bid his bishops to decide only for what might be called the power gospels of Mathew through John for their investment in authority and for some kind of "divine right" of some to rule others and to ban those that might not be very conducive to power by authority, it could be perceived that he and his obedient bishops lifted the meat portion of the pie of life and Jesus and discarded it while saving only the non meat half of the pie.

For comparison purposes, let us say that the non meat portion of the pie is what might be called the Messianic perception of Jesus and life. The meat portion that was eliminated, then, is the **Holistic** perception of Jesus and life. We say something is meaty if it is substantial. To believe that life itself is **meaty** and substantial of itself without need of additional grace is certainly what I would call a **Holistic** view of life.

What is a Messianic perception of life and Jesus? It is a view that holds that mankind has actually been separated from God and needs to be united – or reunited – with God. For that union or reunion, a special emissary from God is needed. That emissary for traditional Christians is Jesus. Jesus, then, came to save mankind from a separation from God and unite – or reunite – mankind with God by virtue of being from God Himself. That is the Messianic view of Jesus and life. That perception of Jesus was retained with all the gospels and epistles that eventually became what is generally referred to as the **New Testament**.

Lost from the discussion, however, has been the **Holistic** view of life and Jesus. What is that? It is the perception that mankind was never separated from God, though it may have thought it has been. Having never been separated from God, then no person or event is necessary to unite – or reunite – mankind with God. Mankind is essentially **holy** as is. That is what I would call the **Holistic** perception of life and Jesus. **The Holistic perception of life is based on the notion that life itself is Divine because God is inside of it, not outside of it.** God has to be **in** life because God is **infinite,** virtually meaning *everywhere.* If God is in life, then life is Divine. It is as simple as that.

The **Holistic** perception was, however, banned by Constantine. Gospels like those of Thomas and Mary were banned along with the condemnation of a **Holistic** view of life and Jesus. It is my view that Jesus was not a **Messianic disciple** of the Jews, but rather a **Holistic apostle** of humanity in general. It has become somewhat clear to me that the Messianic bunch carved Jesus into being one of them; but I do not believe he was one of them because I do not believe that, number 1, a messiah was needed in the first place because there has never been a separation between mankind and God, and, number 2, because it appears clear to me via the Gospels of Thomas and Mary that Jesus, himself, had a **Holistic** perception of life. If Jesus really was of a **Holistic** mind and not a Messianic mind, then how could he have been a messiah?

In the 3rd Verse of what could be called the **Holistic** *GOSPEL OF THOMAS,* Jesus says *If you know yourselves, then you will be known and you will know that you are sons of the Living Father.* This is not the statement of a messiah intent on restoring us to God, but rather the statement of one who believes we are already in God and God is in us. This is a statement about who we are now, not what we might become if, allegedly, we accept Jesus as our personal savior. **We are sons of the Living Father – just like Jesus – and it has nothing to do with Jesus.**

I do not think Jesus came to convert us into something different because we lacked some wholesomeness for lacking God, but rather he came to make us aware of what we are – *sons of the Living Father.* Male and female, we are all sons in this sense because we are all born of the Living Father. There is equality among us all. That is the lesson of Jesus. We have no sin in us by nature because we are divine, although we can sin. **Sin is not a condition. It is an act by which we fail to note our divinity and act accordingly.**

In *THE GOSPEL OF MARY, Peter said to him, "You have explained everything to us. Tell us also, what is the sin of the world?" The savior replied, "There is no such thing as sin, but you create sin when you mingle, as in adultery, and this is called sin."* Indeed, that is sin. It is that which we lack within ourselves, but not that which we lack naturally, but that which we lack, vision wise. It is seeing evil in Nature where there is none. It is powering over others and doing what we please and calling it "God's Will." It is failing to love your enemy for not seeing God within him and calling it "God's Justice" when you kill him. It is being just and killing the infidel and calling it "God's Judgment." It is all these things, but it is not "God's Absence" – for nothing can be absent of God because God is Present in All.

The opposite of sin is kindness to all. Everyone who claims to love Jesus knows that Jesus taught unconditional kindness as the ideal of life; but being kind to one's enemies is impractical. Justice appeals to those who rule. Kindness does not. Justice is practical. Kindness is not. Justice can find advocates among those who believe they are rightful authorities. Justice is good for kings and queens and emperors and religious leaders. Kindness is not very useful for any who love authority. The real Jesus had to be deformed as a prince of kindness and reformed as a chair of judgment in order to work in the world of rulers. No ruler in his right mind could embrace kindness over justice; but just the same, the real Jesus probably advocated kindness over justice. Why? Because, as he said again and again, *my Kingdom is not of this world.*

What is his Kingdom? We are all guessing about that, but my guess is that it is a communion of souls who practice unconditional kindness because all are equal. It is my guess that many qualify for that Kingdom who actually choose kindness to all – whether they are aware of Jesus or not. It is also my guess that many who prefer justice over kindness can never enter the real Kingdom of Jesus – whether they claim Jesus as Lord or not.

That is not to say those excluded by attitude are doomed to Hell. Not at all. Just because one does not earn membership in the Kingdom of Jesus does not mean they won't gain some admission to some degree to what might be called Heaven. Virtually speaking, **Heaven is only being aware of the Presence of God.** I suppose it is possible to be aware of the Presence of God and still not center on kindness to all. That is not for me to judge; and Thank God, I do not have to judge such a matter.

In truth, **judgment is really only continuing what we begin.** It has little to do with another's judgment of you or me. It has mostly to do with our judgment of ourselves – and as we judge ourselves, we will continue. That's judgment. If we are mean, we will continue to be mean – until we stop being mean. That's judgment. If we are kind, we will continue to be kind. That's judgment. If we are non forgiving, we will continue to be non forgiving. That's judgment. If we are champions of justice, ignoring kindness, we will continue to be champions of justice. That's judgment. We decide our course. That's judgment. As we sow, we will reap. It has been said many times that such is so; and it probably is. It makes sense. Doesn't it?

And perhaps the worst kind of judgment may be commitment to law as a way of salvation. This kind of judgment is truly sad because when you commit yourself to a law of salvation, you expect reward for obedience and punishment for disobedience. As you expect, there will be others more than willing to accommodate you; but your reward may not be the reward you expect. Once another gets you into his corral of justice, you may be caught within a web very difficult to escape because you will have no other vision telling you that you have a right to escape. Your judgment may be that you turned over the right to determine your own judgment to others; and when that happens, you may become truly lost – not even recognizing the possibility that you do not deserve what others are handing out.

We covered the idea in a previous essay. In *THE GOSPEL OF MARY,* Jesus said: *Go and preach the good news of the Kingdom. Do not lay down any rules other than what I have given you, and do not establish law, as the law-giver did, or you will be bound by it.* The "good news" was previously offered as seeing the *child of humanity* within us. That was the rule that Jesus laid down – no law – just one rule – to respect the *child of humanity* within us. To violate that rule merely ends in failure to belong to his Kingdom of peace; but there is no punishment by others for violating it.

And then Jesus admonished us not to establish law – which does allow for punishment by others for disobedience – because if we do, we will be bound by the law we embrace. It works that way. If I submit to a law made by you and obey your command because I think you have rightful authority over me – even though you do not have rightful authority – I will still be bound to you because I believe you had the right to be a law-giver. It is this respecting another's right to make law and your responsibility to obey it that may amount to the cruelest judgment of all because by releasing yourself to another's whim, you may be lost in ways that will be hard to escape. How can one escape that which one doesn't think one should escape or has a right to escape?

I think the lawgiver that Jesus was admonishing us about was Moses or any of the like who have listened to other lawgivers, bidding us to obey or suffer penalty for disobedience. Moses had to obey his lawgiver because he believed in him - just like others had to obey Moses because they believed in Moses. Moses thought his law-giver was authentic; and the followers of Moses thought the same. In the end, Moses and his people had to wander about in a desert having sand for desert and sacrifice for entertainment all because they listened to lawgivers that were not from God as they claimed. Jesus was very aware of the danger of submitting to another and getting lost in a sandstorm of another's making. That is why he admonished us to be careful about establishing law. Law can be a trap and the judgment of that trap can be devastating.

Difficult as it might be, however, in the end, it is our choice – freedom by independence from law and respect of the child of humanity within us all – or commitment to law and all its normal consequences; but regardless of any of it, it is all Heaven. Like Jesus says in one of the canonized gospels of the **BIBLE, My Father's house has many mansions.** Heaven is as wide as the world is wide because it is really only the Presence of God; though virtually speaking, it is awareness of the Presence of God. If we are unaware we are in Heaven, though we actually are, virtually speaking, we are not in Heaven; but actually speaking, since God is really everywhere, that makes Heaven also everywhere.

As Jesus says in the 113th Verse of **THE GOSPEL OF THOMAS, the Kingdom of the Father is spread upon the earth and men do not see it.** Again, however, if I am unaware of my being in Heaven, then virtually speaking, though I am really in Heaven, if I think I am in Hell, then Hell will be my home.

In the end, too, by our chosen conduct and attitude, we choose our own communion of souls with whom we wish to assemble. If in life we insist on justice over kindness, then it will be those same kind with whom we will associate in any life to come. The irony of that may be that we may be companions of the ones we killed and they of us because neither of us will recognize it will be our bitterness that will have brought us together.

For sure, the debate will go on – or at least, it should go on. With the discoveries of the previously banned gospels (and still banned by most traditional Christian voices) of Thomas and Mary, the meat portion of the pie can now be returned to the pie of life. In life, Apostles Thomas and Mary Magdalene – alleged authors of the gospels in their names - probably knew Jesus in one way – and Peter and his subordinates, Matthew, Mark, Luke, and John (and Paul) probably knew him in another.

With some degree of confidence, many of us who have come to believe that Thomas and Mary knew Jesus better than did Peter and his subordinates and who have slid off the Messianic ship of life and Jesus to board the *Holistic* ship of life and Jesus can finally get on with resuming our long, long interrupted lives. We have been banned for centuries. The Messianic clans of mankind have held complete power – though there have been a lot of squabbles among them as evidenced by the zillion and one different churches of Messianic Christianity.

What lies in store for **Holistic Christianity**? I hope many will aspire to it and live by its rather easy and simple principle that **Life and God are One**. In the end, it will be to each, his or her own – just like it should be. I hope this little series has been somewhat helpful in the discussion. I know I represent only one small part of a huge discussion. I am no more essential to that discussion than anyone is. Still, I am glad I could be even a small part of that discussion. It is a discussion that is rarely conducted, but is, I believe, a discussion that deserves at least as great attention as the Messianic view of life does.

In my opinion, we live in a world in which we are being suffocated as souls, compared to what it could be. As Jesus may figuratively say it, we are like a flower garden inundated with weeds. The problem is that we can't tell the difference between the weeds and the flowers. Make no mistake about it. There are a heap of flowers in the garden, but there are also a lot of weeds that look like flowers; and the weeds seem to be much stronger than the flowers. That is because they are far more gullible. It is easy to grow a weed because it doesn't take much nutrition. Flowers require more, as it were; and so that is probably the biggest reason the weeds outnumber the flowers in the current world. Ask any weed, though; and you will be told he or she or it thinks it's a flower.

And so it is, too. Be it a weed or a flower, it all comes from God in that God is the source of all existence. For God, a weed is a flower because the same wonderful divine energy that goes into a flower also goes into a weed. It is not from God's point of view that there are weeds. Indeed, for God, there are only flowers; but for those of us souls struggling to make our lives ones of freedom, well, it stands to reason that there cannot be near as much freedom for a flower in a patch of weeds as is in a patch all its own.

In time, perhaps, weeds will disappear. Perhaps souls will choose to be born as flowers, having come to realize that for the sake of free souls, that is the way it is supposed to be. There is no reason why there has to be weeds, suffocating and strangling flowers. When the weeds of the world finally realize their time would be much better spent as flowers, free of strangulation and suffocation, then the flower population will grow; and, who knows, in time, maybe only flowers will exist.

Needless to say, in this series, my opinions have been my own. As I have had my own opinions and have tried to offer some of them, I hope that others will enter the fray on the side of **Holistic Christianity;** and: Together, maybe we can add to a Movement, that interrupted or not, has always been around – and will forever be so.

Song Of My Divine Naturism

By
Francis William Bessler
June/July, 2004

CANTATION:
I'm in love with life and God
as if the two are one.
I have no doubt whatever
that whatever is – is God's son.
God is the Divine –
and Nature is God's Prism.
That's why I call
my wondrous belief "Divine Naturism."

As I watch from a window,
I see a cloud go by.
I'm amazed at it all
and wonder how it can all be so fine.
As I ponder the sun
and its generous sunshine,
I have no doubt in my mind
that all that is – is Divine.

But it is not only life
that has the spark of Divinity, you see.
Even the sand
must contain the wondrous mystery.
For life itself springs from the sand –
as if therein is the seed.
God is present in it all –
just as It is - in you and me.
Cantation.

People ask me, where is God,
and I answer "everywhere."
God is not a person, but rather
a Creative Presence of Infinite Care.
There is nothing that can exist
that can exist on its own.
God is the wonderful principle
by which all that is – is sown.

People have this idea
that when they die they go to God.
But if God is in everything,
then now should begin the applause.
God is not something
that can only come to some of us later.
It must be something that right now
every single being can savor.
Cantation.

And God can't be in the business
of judging me and you
because a judge has to be outside
of that which is viewed.
God is inside of all that is
and therefore cannot be a judge.
That leaves it up to each of us
to live without a grudge.

Judgment is only
having to continue as I begin.
I am my own judge and it is for me
to determine what is sin.
Virtue is only embracing
that which sets my soul free.
So I choose to love all that is
like all that is – is me.
Cantation.

I am asked many things,
but one question is, do I have a soul?
I say I don't know for sure,
but it's only smart to act like it is so.
If I do have a soul,
then it can only serve as a record of me.
It is then up to me
to make sure that I keep that record clean.

Assuming that I have a soul,
it makes sense that I fill that vessel
only with that I'd like to recover –
and for me, that's only the gentle.
Surely, it is to each, his own,
but however we fill our soul,
we will have to inherit later
all that we put into our bowl.
Cantation.

I have but one rule
that I think Jesus tried to get all to mind.
It's really not very complicated.
That single rule is – Be Kind.
Kindness is its own reward
because by being kind, I'm always at peace.
It doesn't matter where I go,
what I do, or who or what I meet.

People tell me that you can't be kind
to those who are unkind.
They say that justice demands
that that they must pay the price.
But being unkind to the unkind
only makes two who are fools.
No one who is wise
would ever attend such a school.
Cantation.

Jesus tried to teach kindness to all
two thousand years ago,
but the rulers of the day
claimed it to be an impossible way to go.
And anyone who would ask it
must be put up on the cross.
Otherwise, they thought, society at large
would reap tremendous loss.

And so it has continued down
through the many, many years.
Justice over kindness
has shed a jillion tears.
And today, mankind still loves
to go to war and fight
and find in their claimed acts of justice
that which they think is right.
Cantation.

The beat goes on. It cannot stop
until mankind stops punishing the kind
and allows the Heaven they want sometime later
to be here in time.
When Jesus said that Heaven is at hand,
he did not mean tomorrow.
If you put off until tomorrow,
all you'll gain is endless sorrow.

Heaven is something that is ours
once we come to realize
that Heaven is only being aware
that everything is Divine.
Life itself can only be a mystery,
but the results of it need never be.
As the twig is bent, so it will grow –
and the twig that grows is only me.
Cantation (2 or 3 times).

Child Of Humanity Series

The End

Exploring

The Soul

and

Brother Jesus

The End

About the Author

Francis William Bessler was born on a small farm outside Powell, Wyoming, on December 3, 1941. The seventh of Leo and Clara Bessler's eight children, Bessler was raised Christian Catholic.

After high school, Bessler spent six years studying for the Catholic ministry, first at St. Lawrence Seminary in Mount Calvary, Wisconsin, and later at St. Thomas Seminary in Denver, Colorado.

In the spring of 1966, Bessler was asked to discontinue his studies as his "thinking was not that of a Catholic priest." Specifically, the seminary objected to his argument that faith must be subject to understanding, without which no dogma could be upheld as truth with any certainty. His dogma professor went so far as to label him heretical. His expulsion didn't stop him from considering the nature between the soul and the divine. If anything, it strengthened his resolve.

More information about Bessler can be found at www.una-bella-vita.com.

Books
by

Francis William Bessler

(Main Theme: Life Is Divine, Sinless, Sacred, & Worthy)

See www.una-bella-vita.com
or enter "Francis Bessler"
in the search bar of Amazon.com
for availability.

Prices vary from $14 to $28 -
depending upon size of book.

1.
WILD FLOWERS
(about 280 pages)
(essays and songs mostly written as website blogs
from 2012 to 2014)
Printed in a smaller font 2 type.

2.

FIVE HEAVEN ON EARTH STORIES
(about 430 pages)
(Featuring 5 philosophical stories
written from 1975 - 2007)
Printed in a larger font 4 type
for the benefit of an easier read.

3.

EXPLORING THE SOUL -
And BROTHER JESUS
(about 200 pages)
(Featuring an analysis of several theories
about the origin and destiny of the soul -
and supplying an original idea too -
originally written in 1988.
Also, featuring a new look at Jesus
via an essay series written in 2005)
Printed in a larger font 4 type
for the benefit of an easier read.

4.

JOYFUL HAPPY SOUNDS!
(about 500 pages)
(featuring all of my songs and poems
written from 1963 to 2015 - total: 197)
Printed in a smaller font 2 type.

5.
LOVING EVERYTHING
(WILD FLOWERS # 2)
(about 270 pages)
(essays and songs mostly written as website blogs
from 2014 to 2015)
Printed in a smaller font 2 type.